tears of a mother:

a sudanese survivor's story

By Abeny Kucha Tiir

Edited by Susan A. Miller
Copyedited and designed by CreateSpace
Lincoln, Nebraska
November 2011

Kirkus Indie Review

Debut author Tiir presents a heart-rending account of her family's flight from war in Sudan to a new life in the United States.

Tiir's pleasant childhood segued into a period of turmoil and danger as Sudan became engulfed in civil war. Her family decided to leave their village to try to find safety elsewhere. Life became a series of moves from refugee camp to refugee camp in Ethiopia, Kenya and back to Sudan, often just steps ahead of marauding government soldiers and rebels. During this journey, Tiir's husband, brother and daughter died, but in the struggle to keep herself and her growing family alive, she had no time to grieve. She was often blessed to find a relative, stranger or some lucky break that allowed her to carry on while her faith was tried and tested, calcifying in the extreme hardship. They went without food for so long, her youngest children forgot how cake tasted; they went without water for so long, her children's tongues swelled to the point that water couldn't trickle down their throats. These dire, subhuman circumstances continued until Tiir was able to fill out paperwork that allowed her family to start a journey toward immigration to the U.S. Gaps in her story—particularly after the family arrives in the U.S.—sometimes make it hard to follow. Filling in those empty spaces would create a more complete, compelling portrait of their journey. Elsewhere, Dinka tribal customs need to be explained in greater detail to help readers understand why Tiir was constantly shifting her children to other people and, likewise, why other people were passing children to her for are. Tiir's memoir ends on an optimist note: She found a church and a career and, in Nebraska, is surrounded by generous people. Someday she'd like to return to Sudan, which one hopes has a better future ahead, too.

A heartbreaking yet triumphant story of faith, family and survival.

Kirkus Indie, Kirkus Media LLC, 6411 Burleson Rd., Austin, TX 78744
indie@kirkusreviews.com

Epigraphs

I was about to cook and then these rumors came. Sometimes I am the first to decide to leave. Even if people were thinking no, there is nothing that is going to happen. They said that I was always the one who wanted to go—to leave—to die moving. To die on the go instead of die staying in one place.

-My family.

-Atong's graduation at St. Thomas Law school in St. Paul, Minnesota.

Dedicated to:

To my brother Jok Mathayo Kucha Tiir, my husband
Akech Jok Kut Jok, and our daughter Aduot Akech Jok Kut Jok

-My husband.

-My daughter Aduot, to whom the book is dedicated to (to the left)

Acknowledgments

Nancy Lutein, who helped me find a place to live when I moved to Lincoln.

All the churches that helped me when I moved to the U.S.: Episcopal Church of Portland, Maine; Calvary Episcopal Church in Rochester, Minnesota; United Methodist Church in Lewisville Nebraska; Bible Church, St. Charles, Minnesota.

Dr. Mary Pipher

Father Nicklaus Mezacapa

Dr. Greg and Kim Wiseman

Dr. Randy and Julie Roegnik

Bob and Jinny Padzieski

Frank and Dottie Hawthorne

Joan Kiple(My very good teacher).

ST.John Cathulic Church in Rochester Minnesota.

Mary Vlazny

Dr. Hal and Elaine Wente.

Jerry Freetly.

Luthren Church in Rochester Minnesota.

Bruce and Cheri Struve.

Melvin Alms.

Calvary Community Church in Lincoln Nebraska.

Pastor Carl and Gayle Godwin.

Barb Vanderbeek.

Leisa Larson.

Robrenna Redl.

Zaineb Garang.

Abeny Kuol Tiir.

Contents

Introduction

I have walked through hell holding the hand of God. My life has been a painful miracle, but not without light. My story is a reflection of the tragedy of Africa, a continent of beauty and sorrow. So severe is Africa's contrast that each person born into its grace must fight for his or her own survival.

For many years, Sudan, my homeland, was wracked by civil war between north and south. The Muslims in the North held most of the power and were using force to convert the indigenous people and Christians in the South to Islam. The government arbitrarily displaced people from their villages, separating families and friends. Rebels from the South mounted a rebellion that lasted for years. The government would respond to rebel activity by bombing villages of innocent people. These conditions forced many people to flee Sudan to refugee camps in Kenya and Ethiopia. My new husband and I did just that in 1986.

My husband and my brother joined the fight to protect our people and died as heroes. My baby daughter died of starvation and disease. I was left as a young woman, abandoned by fate. My other children looked to me for their lives. My story is of how I found the strength to survive and how faith was born out of despair. The greatest instinct of human nature is to protect oneself and one's family. I have done many things to protect my children. I could not give up hope when the hope was my children. This is my story told from a heart scarred, but beating with love for all I have now and those I left behind. I know that God will heal my heart of its wounds.

Many women who read this will wonder if they would have the strength to live my story. Let them learn from my story that God gives us strength that we may not know we have.

Who am I to write a book? I don't even speak good English, and I cannot write very well. I wrote this book so people would know what I went through, because I believe my story can help others. God gives wisdom in many different forms, so I used the wisdom that God gave me and found my own way of "writing" a book.

All I did was tape-record a story that's in my heart. I found a quiet time in my house and prepared myself. Then I turned on the tape recorder and talked into it. Sometimes I felt like an idiot doing that, but I continued. As soon as I heard a sound in the house, I turned off the tape and waited until the next day. When I did it in a quiet place, everything just came in order the exact way it happened. When I came to traumatic memories, I cried and talked into the tape while I was crying. The tape recorded my grieving voice, my sad voice, my angry voice, my happy voice… That's why I did it alone when the house was very quiet.

At a conference in San Jose, California, I met Cathy Parr of Wyoming, who began the typing of this manuscript. Later, Pastor Carl Godwin of Calvary Community Church in Lincoln, Nebraska, introduced me to Mary Rittenburg, who completed the typing. After I had a typed manuscript, I needed an editor. Algis Laukaitis at the Lincoln Journal Star had written an article about how Habitat for Humanity had built me their hundredth Lincoln house. I asked him to help me. He passed my request along, and a freelance editor, Susan Miller, phoned me. Susan and I are both from tribes; I am a Dinka and she is a Seminole. Therefore, Susan charged me the "Indian price" for her editorial work. That got us off to a good start. I was finally able to relax and expect a good outcome for this project. We met regularly and revised the manuscript. I kept praying for help and thanking God for what came.

Chapter 1:
Before the War

I was born into a Christian family. My father's name is Mathayo Kucha Tiir. My mother was called Adau Thiel Lual. She came from the Lual Deng family, known as Pan Lual from Dak Chuek in northern Bor. They a strong and brave people, well known as warriors and heroes among the Bor tribes.

Kuchdok, My Natal Village in Bor Province, Southern Sudan

I was born in a small village called Kuchdok (pronounced KWIHdah) on the eastern bank of the White Nile in a southern area of Bor Province called Paleek. This area lies in Bor South County, Jonglei State, South Sudan. My simple childhood was a happy one. I was surrounded by family and friends. I went to school and learned many things. Although I was raised Christian, my father had four wives as is the custom in my country. I lived among many brothers and sisters. There has always been disruption in Africa, but in my village much of my life was happy. I had enough food, and I lived comfortably with my mother, brothers, and sisters.

When I was an infant, too young to remember, my people's traditional marks were cut into my forehead. It was done to me for healing. Marking is done on foreheads or temples of babies and toddlers as a way of healing eye problems. It is also done for beauty at about the age of ten. My people, the Dinka Bor, cut six long marks into the center of the forehead: three to one side and three to the other. Each group of Dinka has its own mark. My father said the Dinka Bor mark might have been adopted from the Mendari tribe.

I also have a large scar on my front upper right thigh because when I was born people came from towns to immunize children. My mom had gone to get water when I was immunized. It was just a shot, perhaps for measles, but it got infected, as often happened, and left a large scar.

I was aware at a very young age of conflicts pertaining to religion. My uncle was a priest, and my father stood beside him as a fellow Christian. In my village many of the natives still worshiped idols, snakes, and other tokens of false gods. When my uncle burned many of these items, it led my family into making enemies in the village.

From Kuchdok to Leer in Bantiu Province

When I was very young, we moved to a village called Leer (pronounced Lehr) in the province of Bantiu. Leer was a village of people of the Nuer tribe. We are not Nuers, but my father took a job there with the health department. Many people there lived according to Nuer tradition. I still speak the Nuer language.

I don't exactly know my birthday. In the Sudan records on such things are very sparse. In America birthdays are such a celebration. In Africa each birth is met with joy, but each birth is an added responsibility for life. We kept track of a child's age partly by the loss of baby teeth and the growth of permanent teeth.

My father was a man who believed in education. When I was six years old, he took me to school in Leer with my sister on registration day. I think the Sudanese government ran the school. Children started school at seven years, but because no birth records were kept, teachers checked for permanent teeth to determine whether a child was old enough to start school. A child with baby teeth was considered too young and was sent home. On the first day, the children lined up, and a teacher checked each child's teeth. My sister was seven or eight years old, and the teacher accepted her, but he pushed me aside and told me I could not stay.

I started to cry and scream. I wanted to go to school that badly. I threw myself onto the floor, crying and screaming. My father tried to calm me down, explaining that I could come back next year. I would not be calmed. After all the other children with baby teeth had gone home, I was still there, crying, and insisting that I be allowed to stay. Finally the teacher told my father that it would be all right for me to stay with my sister. The teacher made my sister share her notebook with me. He cut it into two parts. My sister did not like sharing her notebook, but I was allowed to stay.

After the first three months, we took an exam called the *small exam*. I passed it. I even made one hundred percent in math. The teacher told my father that it would be all right for me to continue in school. I was very happy about that. After that, my sister and I helped each other. I helped her with math, and she helped me with the Arabic language. I liked school very much and was an excellent student.

From Leer to the Town of Bantiu

After first grade, we moved from Leer to the town of Bantiu. It was a larger town, and we children were happy to go there. We could get bread there, and we children all loved the bread. I started second grade there, and there I met Muslims for the first time. The teachers were from the north, and some were Egyptians. Our math teacher was an Egyptian man.

In Bantiu, I began to see the conflict between Muslims and Christians. The headmaster announced that all the girls would have to cover their heads. I told my mom that we needed to cover our heads. I did not understand, but my mother told me that it was an Islamic rule, not a Christian rule, but that we would have to follow it. She bought me a scarf to wear. The school uniform was green and the scarf had to be white. We got in trouble if the scarf slipped from our heads.

They taught Muslim religion in this school. We were forced to study the Koran every day. I still can read the Koran in Arabic. The girls and boys were kept separate within the school. This did not seem to be a problem for us, but as Christians we were treated much differently than the Muslims. For an hour a day, the school taught the Christian religion to Christian students and Islam to the Muslim students. I remember that the Christian girls were made to go outside in the heat and sit under a tree for that hour, even though we were the majority. We did not fight with the Muslim girls because we knew it was we who would get into trouble and be beaten by the teachers.

School was much better in third grade because our teacher was Christian. We got to have the girls and boys mixed. Our teacher was fun. He made a game of getting the right answer. If he called on a boy who answered the question incorrectly, a girl who got the answer correct got to slap the boy. Later in the day on the way home, the boys who had gotten slapped tried to hit us back. The teacher got in terrible trouble for starting this game.

After my father moved us to Bantiu, he left us there and moved back to Bor. Bor was his home town, and his first wife lived there. It is not uncommon for a husband to leave one wife and her children and live with another wife in a different town. A woman has a choice about where to live. A husband provides for each household. Multiple wives do not usually live in the same house. Grown children help their mother, and thus she does not depend on her husband and does not mind sharing with a second wife. My uncle had nine wives. They got along by being polite to each other.

Teeth Extraction and Facial Marking

In 1974, when I was about eight or ten years old, my mom took us to Bor on vacation. I found that my friends in Bor were having their two lower front permanent teeth removed because they believed it made them beautiful. This was a common Dinka practice, performed in summer on children when they were around nine or ten years old. My auntie asked me, "Can you let your teeth be removed?" I said no.

The woman who removed teeth came to my stepmother's house to remove the teeth of my two girl cousins. People believed that this woman's hands had been blessed and that the blessing would prevent bad results from any operation that she performed. The woman kept her teeth-extracting implements in a carrying case made of a lightweight wood whose center was carved out. It was perhaps a yard long, ten inches wide, and ten inches tall. In it she also carried her smoking tobacco and coins. She used it as a stool to sit on, and when there was a dance, she would carry it as she danced.

Many Dinka people, mostly men, carried such cases and would dance with them, sit on them, use them as pillows, and carry things in them. People outside the Dinka world did not recognize that these objects were carrying cases that might hold valuable items, and therefore the cases were rarely stolen.

When the woman came to my stepmother's home to remove the children's teeth, some of my relatives insisted that I allow her to remove mine. Some of my female relatives held me down for her, but my brothers rescued me. I had also avoided the removal of my baby teeth, a traditional Dinka medical practice, believed to prevent teething pain. Thus I have kept all my teeth.

According to Dinka tradition, children's foreheads were marked in the early teen years. After a girl's first menstrual period and the appropriate ceremony, she could choose decorative marks on her forehead and/or stomach. Similarly, boys might get marks on their foreheads and/or shoulders. The marking might be done on the same occasion as the extraction of teeth, or it might be done a year later. To prevent infections, parents would have the operations done at a time when few flies were around, and the weather was good. A good child would ask the permission of a parent or responsible adult to have teeth removed and forehead marked. When my younger sister had her teeth removed, our father was angry because she had not asked his permission.

Cattle Camps

Marking was usually done in cattle camps, because that is where a child of that age was usually staying. Cattle camps played a major role in Dinka family life because of the importance of cattle to a family's economy. A Dinka family's wealth was measured not in money but in cattle. Wealth was having many cows. Cattle, goats, and sheep were comparable to a savings account. You did not eat them up. Eating of herd animals was done only at special times, such as weddings, funerals, and visits by special guests. Otherwise, if you wanted meat, you would go hunting. Although cattle camps were a feature of village life, a Dinka who lived in town might buy cattle and add them to his or her family's herd in the village.

My life was unusual in that I lived in both town and village. Life in the village was still much like my people's ancestral way of life. A family kept its cattle near the village during the rainy season, but moved them to cattle camps on the other side of the Nile in February for the hot dry summer. Fresh water and tall grass were plentiful there on the other side. Young people would explore the other side of the river to find good places for a camp. Then older people in the family would decide where the camp would be. When the rains began in late March or early April, the family would move the cattle back to the village.

Sometimes we kept the cattle in three groups. One herd was kept far away from the village where grass and water were best. They would be retrieved only when needed for a dowry. (Dowries were paid in cattle. The groom's family would give cattle to the bride's family. A family with only sons had a problem.) Young married couples stayed with this herd, along with young girls and boys. A second herd was kept nearer the village, and the third group of animals was kept in the village to provide milk for the elderly, who were the only people left in the village through this season.

All young people were supposed to take care of the animals, so everyone would spend time in cattle camps growing up. Children would be taken to the camps soon after their weaning at the age of two. People in the camp also included men and women in their thirties and forties who supervised the young people. A camp leader would be elected in a meeting of the camp's men. Boys took care of calves, and young men took care of older cows. Girls milked cows, made yogurt and butter, cooked, and took care of young children. Thus cattle camps played a major role in traditional child rearing.

When a woman married, she would go to live with her husband's family. Then during her first pregnancy, usually during her seventh or eighth month, her father would ask her husband's father to allow her to return to her parents' home for the baby's birth. She would stay with her parents until the baby was weaned. Ideally, a baby would be weaned to cow's milk. Therefore, the child would be moved to the mother's family's cattle camp where milk was readily available. A female relative would take the newly weaned child to the camp while the baby's mother returned to live with her husband's family. At the cattle camp, a child had access to the best possible diet: not only milk products, but also fresh fish, game, and other nutritious foods.

When the child was about seven years old, the father would ask the mother's father to permit the child to leave the cattle camp and go to the father's home to start school or begin training in traditional Dinka economic pursuits. In a traditional Dinka household, boys learned to hunt and care for goats, sheep, and cows. Girls learned women's skills such as keeping house, cooking, and entertaining guests. The mother's relatives provided food to accompany the child from the cattle camp to the father' home in the village of the paternal grandparents.

From the Town of Bantiu to Bor

My mother and her children were living in the town of Bantiu, and my father was living with his first wife in Bor. He would visit us in Bantiu. My father loved me very much and wanted me to continue learning after I finished elementary school. On one of his visits he saw that I was working a lot and doing a lot of babysitting. He thought I was being worked too hard and had no time to learn, so he took me to Bor with him. I was about thirteen years old.

I lived with my stepmother, Anyeth Jur Bior, in Bor, and my mother stayed in Bantiu for about a year and then moved to Bor. My mother did not like living in town, so she moved back to Kuchdok, my birthplace, about nine miles away. I would walk to Kuchdok every weekend to be with her and walk back to Bor to go back to school on Monday morning.

My Brother Jok

Before my sisters were born it was my four brothers and me. I was the only girl in the middle of the boys. My baby brother, Jok, came after me. Jok and I played together a lot. He was a strong boy. I couldn't mess with him because sometimes he would beat me up even though he was younger than me. I tried to be nice to him all the time, and he protected me from more aggressive children.

I started school first, and then later we were in elementary school together. Then we moved from Leer to Bantiu and continued our elementary school education until fourth grade. Then, when my father moved me back to Bor, Jok stayed with my mother. I finished fifth grade in Bor. The next year my whole family moved to Bor, and Jok and I went to sixth grade together; he in the boys' school and I in the girls'.

When I was in about sixth grade, my stepmother moved to a different house, leaving us children in her house. It was just Jok and me and some of our cousins, but no adults. Some of our older relatives would come by to check on us, but that did not happen every day. I do not know why the adults decided to arrange it that way. It was very difficult for us. Jok and I woke up every morning and went to school. Boys and girls attended separate schools four or five blocks apart. After school we came back and played. He was a very strong boy, and when some of my stepsisters would try to do something to him, he would fight them. Even though he was younger, he would beat them up. I kept my mouth shut because I didn't want him to beat me up.

After sixth grade, I needed a boarding school because my mother lived so far away, and my stepmother had moved out of the house. Even though I was too young my father convinced a boarding school to let me attend. I was accepted and moved in with an older girl whom I grew to love. So I attended middle school—seventh through ninth grades—in this boarding school.

Jok went to a boys' middle school, which was also a boarding school. During these years, he and I grew even closer. We walked together and hung out together. We often held hands and were hugging each other all the time. Sometimes we even slept together on the floor on plastic sheets, and we covered ourselves with traditional handmade sheets. This kind of innocent closeness is common between young Sudanese brothers and sisters. He was my lovely brother until we went on to high school.

When we became teenagers and went to high school we sometimes made fun of each other. We teased each other, especially during the ceremonies when I became a woman and he became a man.

Girl's Coming-of-Age Ceremony

At the time of my first menstrual period, I went through my people's traditional ceremonies. When you first began menstruating, you didn't go to your mom's house, you went to your father's brother's house and told one of your uncle's wives about what had happened to you. Then one of your uncle's wives would go and tell other women, and you had a ceremony.

One woman, often a relative of the girl's family, would be chosen to sponsor the ceremony. Later, the girl's family would reward the sponsor and any of the sponsor's friends who had helped her with the ceremony. They might give her a goat or other things that she needed. At the wedding ceremony, the sponsor would receive something—perhaps a metal bracelet—to show that she had taken responsibility for the things that needed to be done at the time of the bride's first menstruation. Everyone respected her, and she would be treated like a special person.

The sponsor and the uncle's wives picked the day of the ceremony, usually one to two weeks later. They wouldn't let you go to your mom, because they said that if you stepped on your mom's foot during that time, or she stepped on your foot, she would stop having babies. You must not step where your mom walked, and she must not step where you walked. So they kept you away from your mom until the day of the ceremony. Then in a ceremony called the Foot Reunion, your feet and your mom's feet were reunited. So I was kept in my uncle's house for two weeks until the ceremony.

Two or three months later, if you were the first daughter of your biological mother, there was a big celebration. They would kill a lamb, and a group of young women and girls would perform a play. All this ceremony was embarrassing to me, but it was a tradition.

The play was a mock wedding in which the girl honoree was getting married. One of the girls played the part of the groom. Everyone in the village sat in a circle outdoors, the men on one side and the women and girls on the other. The men divided themselves into two groups facing each other, one group representing the bride's family, and the other the groom's. The two groups of men discussed the dowry that the groom's family would provide to the bride's. The groom's men said how many cows they would pay. The bride's men could reject that offer and a negotiation would follow. Everyone else listened to the negotiation until the two groups came to terms. Then the groom's men cut tall grass into pieces, each piece representing a cow. Usually the number of animals represented was one hundred or two hundred. The groom's men divided the cows among the members of the bride's family. Even the bride's family's dogs and cats might receive cows if the groom's family was wealthy. Then everyone would be happy and would start to dance.

It was such a celebration when you became a woman in my village! I was my mom's first daughter, so they had to do that traditional ceremony. Sometimes the boys would hear about a girl's celebration. A girl was forbidden to hit a boy when she had just turned into a woman, because it was believed that the boy's breasts might grow bigger. Therefore, the boys did not want to be near a girl when she was having the celebration. So my brother was trying to make fun of me and telling me, "Don't hit me. Don't touch me." I kept telling him to shut up and not talk to me. There were some traditions for boys too, so I waited for his turn to come.

Boy's Coming-of-Age Ceremony

—A cow hut—one of the largest buildings in the village

When a boy was around twelve or thirteen years old, he could decide to become a man, or his parents could decide that for him. Men could not go just anywhere and do all the things that boys could do. Men could not go to the kitchen and get food to eat. They were to be served by somebody. They could not eat while they were standing around outdoors. They had to eat indoors where nobody could see them. A boy who was becoming a man would go and sit in a special house with twenty or thirty other boys who were becoming men. Then his mother or his sister or some other woman in the family would bring food to him. The boys who were becoming men were shy and embarrassed about these changes in their status.

When a boy thought he was ready to be a man, he would tell his father, and the father would decide whether the boy was ready to follow the rules of manhood. A boy must be able to do what a man needed to do. Boys could do a lot of things that men could not do. When boys milked cows, they could just grab the nipple and put some milk in their mouths, and they could drink milk any time they wanted to. Boys could cook. They could eat while they were walking around. But when they became men, they could no longer do such things. Therefore, they needed to be sure that when they became men, they would obey the rules and respect them. Otherwise, they would embarrass themselves and their families.

The ceremony for boys was conducted by one of the old ladies. That old lady was considered blessed, because she had already been through a lot. It was her job to do this for the boys who were becoming men. Twenty or thirty boys who were turning into young men would gather in that old lady's cow hut. A cow hut is one of the largest buildings in the village. It is built to house the cattle of a household. Most households have their own cow huts.

The boys' families would cook food every day and take it to that hut. The boys stayed in the old lady's cow hut for a month. On the first day, they went there, lined up, and took their clothes off if they were wearing any. (The boys in the village were already completely naked, but boys from town would be clothed.) Then the old lady went down the line and shaved their heads with a razor. Next, she poured some milk on their heads, and then they were men.

They had to be totally naked. All of them were naked and had their heads shaved, and they all stay in the old lady's cow hut for the entire month. Whenever they left the hut, they stayed together and walked in a line. Each of them carried a long stick. When you saw them, you got out of the way because otherwise they thought they could do anything they wanted because they were men now. They could beat up anybody. You just got out of their way.

When my brother decided to go to the village to undergo the ceremony, I told him not to do it because he was going to be naked. He kept telling me to shut up. When he was naked in front of me, it was my turn to make fun of him. I was the one who was going to cook for him while he was in that lady's house, so I went to the village with him.

On that first morning, I took the food in after his head was shaved off. I saw him naked and with no hair, and I kept laughing. He kept telling me I had better shut up. I didn't want him to be mad at me, because he was my good brother, and I respected him. I took food every morning. I cooked special food, so when I arrived all the young men— you couldn't call them boys any more—were very happy because it was different food than what they could eat in the village, and they told me how good it was. They called me a school girl. When they saw me coming, they would say, "Oh my! The school girl is coming with the very good food." So the young men liked me. My brother was happy with me because I made the good food, and the boys liked him because I brought such good food. He told me later about how they talked to him about me. I was glad he was giving me credit.

Back in Bor

When he was done, he was a man, and we went back to town and lived with our stepmother and continued our education. We went to senior secondary school (like grades ten through twelve) at the same school. Unlike earlier grades, this school taught boys and girls together for the first time. He was in a different class, but we were in the same school. We would still meet at lunch, and we would laugh and talk. Later in the afternoon we would come home together. He would see some boys trying to talk to me, and he would tell them to just "bury themselves" if they came and talked to me. Some of them were afraid of him, and they would tell me that he was being really mean and wouldn't let any of them talk to me. They said, "Who would want to marry you?" I told them he was just like that.

When we would get home he would ask me if I had talked to any of them, and I would say that I had not. He said that if they talked to me, he would kill them. He did not want any boy from school to talk to me. I did not like that, but I could not tell him without causing a big fight. This is how it was with brothers. It is a rule that a girl "stays clean," that is, remains a virgin, until a man comes and officially marries her. We had some fun in high school and were happy with each other sometimes.

Chapter 2:
Kuchdok and the Outbreak of War

The month of May has been engraved in my mind as a month when terrible things happen. Much of the horror in my life started in the month of May. In May 1983 the first frightening episode of violence came to Bor Town. It began as an ordinary spring day. My stepmother sent me to the butchery to buy meat. The only grocery in the town was about half a mile from my home. When I arrived there, many women, girls, and boys were waiting for the butcher to arrive with the fresh meat. Baskets were raised above heads while people chatted and yelled for the butcher to sell them meat. It was very noisy. Then suddenly the sharp report of gunshot filled the air. That was the first shot of the war; it all began in Bor Town.

In their surprise people hit the ground or began to run. I chose to run. I ran blindly, people falling around me. My heart was full of fear as I fought the panic that threatened to overtake my body. There was an old man ahead of me. He grabbed my arm and pulled me aside to a space away from the chaos. My heart was beating loudly with fear. He pulled me hard and told me to lie down. As we lay low breathing the dust of the hot ground, he whispered in my ear asking where I was going. In my fear I had become disoriented, and I told him I did not know how to get home.

There have been many times in my life that death should have covered me in its blackness. This was the first time that I was delivered from death. That old man helped me up and ran with me in the direction of my home. We ran together until my stepmother's hut was in sight.

Once my savior knew I was headed in the right direction, he veered off to find his own safety. In that moment I saw him fall. I wanted to go to him, but my stepmother grabbed me and screamed that there was no time. We had to go now. Gathering a few possessions we ran toward the jungle.

My entire family—my two brothers, my step brother, my sister, and my father and stepmother—all left Bor Town and walked through the jungle to reach my village, Kuchdok, where my real mother lived. We stayed with my mother in Kuchdok for two months until it was safe to go back home to Bor Town. Staying in Kuchdok was not easy, because a government airplane kept flying overhead looking for rebels to bomb. It was the custom of the people of Kuckdok to go naked, so our clothing attracted attention. The villagers were afraid that we would attract a bombing, so they asked my father to allow us children to go naked, but he refused.

After two months we returned to Bor. Cars with microphones drove through the villages announcing that the situation in Bor Town was normal now, so people with jobs and children in school should return to the city. We walked the seven miles back to Bor. Along the way, we met people who told us that things in Bor were not really so good. It was especially dangerous for girls, who were being assaulted by soldiers. Our brothers left us girls along the road so they could investigate the situation there. They found soldiers living in our home in Bor, so we went to our uncle's home. Our uncle said the situation was really bad there. His next door neighbor had been killed the day before. Therefore, he sent six of us girls to stay together in a single hut. We were all about seventeen years old. The older women stayed in a second hut. My uncle had his own hut. The boys stayed in a fourth hut. And a fifth hut was for cooking. The entire compound was inside a fence called a *gate*.

We had been at my uncle's home for only about an hour when soldiers came. Two of them came to the girls' hut, and we six hid under the bed. One of the men called us prostitutes and ordered us to come out from under the bed. He demanded to see our student identifications. My sister and I had ours, but our cousins did not, so he kept threatening them and saying, "I know you are prostitutes, because you have no IDs to show that you are students." After an hour of this, we heard gunfire, and the two men in our rooms left us and ran away along with the other soldiers who had been threatening our uncle and mothers and brothers. The gunfire went on for a couple of hours.

We all gathered in my uncle's hut and shared information about what the soldiers had said and done. My uncle heard all our reports and described his own experience. He advised us about how to avoid trouble in that kind of situation. Especially, he said, we were to be careful not to argue with or antagonize the soldiers.

We learned the next morning that a lot of people had been killed inside a nearby gate. The reason for the massacre was that a member of that family had been an officer in the government's army, but he had deserted to join the rebels. The soldiers found his uniform at his family's home and killed them all.

We went back to Kuchdok for two weeks until the situation became more settled in Bor. When we returned, the soldiers were gone from our house, but they had taken everything we owned. We resumed our life in Bor, but the situation remained unsettled and dangerous.

My Brother Goes to War

By early 1984 the situation in Bor and throughout southern Sudan had become so bad that many people, especially young people, were deciding to leave to join the rebels in Ethiopia. All the young people I knew were very interested in going. My brother Jok was one of them. He wanted to fight. He wanted to get some training to get into the army.

Jok came home from school one day in the afternoon and started chasing me around. We ran around outside the hut, teasing each other and accusing each other of having bed bugs. I thought it was a normal day, but Jok knew that it was not. He must have wanted to create a happy memory of this day. Later I saw a bag in his hand and I asked what it was. He made me promise that I would not tell anyone and then said he was leaving the country.

He was only sixteen, and I was eighteen. He was my baby brother. I told him that only men should go and fight. He said, "I am only sixteen, but I am a man. Don't tell anyone that I am leaving."

I started to look sad. I said, "What if something happens to you?" He said that nothing would happen to him, but if something did, he was a man. He reminded me of elementary school, when only the classes for Muslim girls were allowed to meet inside the classroom, while the classes for Christian girls had to meet outside under the trees in the heat and wind. I told him I remembered, and he said that was why he was going. He said if Jesus died for us, he could die for Jesus. That's what my brother told me. I didn't know what else to say but told him to be careful.

I sold my two dresses and bought a big bag and some peanuts and candies. I gave them to him in his room that night and told him that he was to take them and eat them on the way. I wanted him to be careful, and I wanted him to come back. We hugged and kissed and he told me again that I was not to tell our parents. I promised I would not. He told me to promise that I would not come after him. Girls were leaving the country too, but I promised that I would not leave. He made me promise that I would marry a good husband, and I told him I would. I promised him those three things. He left early in the morning, around three o'clock.

Two days passed, and still no one had noticed that Jok was not there. After about a week, my stepmother noticed, and people started asking me about him. I told everyone that I did not know where he had gone. A month later, rumors filled the village that some of the young people had left to go to fight for freedom. Then my mother and the others in the village understood where he had gone.

A year later disturbing rumors arrived. The news reached my stepmother that Jok had been killed. No one told me. Everyone else in the house knew about it, but my uncle told them not to tell me until he could come himself. Everyone was worried that I might collapse or kill myself, because he was my baby brother, and we were close. I saw everyone in the family lying down and looking sick. All day I kept asking them if they were sick and why they didn't get up. They told me nothing was wrong. They knew what had happened, but I did not know until three o'clock in the afternoon.

I was inside the hut and my uncle called my name. He was sitting outside under the tree. I came out and he held my hand and told me that Jok had been killed. I threw myself down and he held me and took me to his house. I went to bed and would not get up. My father was not there; he had traveled to a different town. When my father heard about it, he came to my uncle's house and found me there. He told me to sit up on the bed. I was only eighteen years old. I sat up and he told me that my Mom was a good mother and had twelve children. None of the children did stupid things or were retarded or wimps. He told me that he wanted me to let Jok go. That's what he told me. He told me to be strong and let him go. He told me to pray. He said that the next morning we would go to the village to see my mom.

The next morning my father came and got me and we walked the long way to the village. It was a lot of walking. In the afternoon we reached the village and my mom saw me coming. She ran to me and she hugged me and we all fell down. My father tried to grab both of us, and some of the villagers came and picked us up. We went to the hut and we were all crying. My mother asked me if I was ready to be strong. I told her I was. My brother was one of the first ones killed in this war.

Marriage

In 1985 when I was about nineteen years old, I was taking the final high school exam, which would conclude my education. The teacher who was supervising us was a handsome and very friendly man named Akech Jok Kut. As we were taking the exam, he was suppose to be watching the classroom to make sure everyone was honest and working. Instead he kept standing by my desk. He was paying too much attention to me. I smiled as I took the test because I knew he was interested in me.

There was a tradition call *alokthok*. When a young woman got married, her sisters and female cousins would accompany her to her new home at the groom's parents' house. Male relatives of the groom would give goats to all these female relatives of the bride. According to the tradition, a female relative of the bride could not eat there until she had received her gift goat. Each of the groom's male relatives would choose which of the girls would receive his goat. If the man liked the girl, he could ask her for a date. If she liked him, she could date him, but she did not have to.

I was out of town when my cousin got married. Later, when I returned to town, Akech insisted on providing the goat for me so that I could eat and drink at my cousin's home. Akech was supposed to come and talk to me at my home about the settlement of the goat. Instead he kept telling me he liked me. I never got the goat. This was the man I was soon to marry. We were married in 1985 when I was nineteen and he was approximately twenty-six.

In accordance with our tribal custom, we lived with my husband's mother in their village, Angakuie ["ng" pronounced as in "sing"], also known as Bideet. My husband's father died before he was born; that is what the name Akech signifies. His mother was blind. My mother-in-law lived at the home of my husband's step-brother.

In accordance with our custom, I arrived at my new home with my cousin Auwr after dark so that nobody would see me. We stood by the side of the hut, my cousin and I, and waited for someone to come out to greet us. When my husband's niece Amor came out, we asked to go inside and sit down. Akech's step-brother Kuol, the head of the household, asked us, "Are you the guests who are leaving or the guests who would like to stay?" We said we were the guests who would like to stay, so he told Amor, his daughter, to make a place for us and get us some water to wash our feet. Then she showed us to the girls' hut, where we were to sleep. Because this was not an arranged marriage, Akech stayed with friends and did not show himself to his family.

The next morning, my husband's mother arrived to greet us. She offered us both her hands and we returned the two-handed greeting. This gesture is a way of showing respect for important guests. She told us we were welcome there. After she left, Kuol came in and greeted us with two hands. Then Kuol's wife Kuie came to greet us with her daughters Amor, Ajak, and Ding. Many women came to greet us and help the family with the cooking. We were not allowed to leave the house. We could not be seen by people outside the family. At long last, at four o'clock in the afternoon, the entire family gathered, and Kuol came into the hut and told us we could come out. Akech's eight uncles performed a ceremony that introduced us into the spiritual body of the community. After that was done, we could eat.

The entire procedure was more complicated than it might have been because the marriage had not been arranged by our elders. Akech's family had to decide whether to accept me as his wife. I had been promised to another man, so my father was angry with Akech and me, and my new husband's family was reluctant to cross my father. (A year passed before my father forgave us.)

In May 1985 I was happy because I had married my husband, but our situation was still very distressful. Food and transportation were scarcely available. Educated people were in much danger because the government thought they were trouble. A rumor reached our village that all educated people must leave or risk being killed by government soldiers. Educated people had already been driven from Bor, so my husband had run out of options. When we met, he had been planning to go to Egypt to further his education, but now war had cut his dreams short. He decided he must go to Ethiopia and join the rebels.

I watched as my husband slipped out of my life and into the darkness of war. This was an awful part of my life. I was pregnant with our first child. The land was in a dark famine, and there was no water. We decided I must move back in with my parents in Kuchdok until the baby was born.

Kuchdok and the Year of Apar

—Teaching my grandson, Malachi, how we carry
babies in South Sudan.

This part of the story is very difficult in my heart. This is the first time I have ever told about it. It was a long time ago, but it still hurts. My first baby, a girl named Atong, was born March 3, 1986, within the first year of my marriage. Even though she was a girl, my husband was not disappointed.

When Atong was only a month old, my mother and I set out for the cattle camps. We knew we would find water there. It was very dangerous for the baby. My mom went back to Kuchdok the next day, and I stayed at the camp with my baby, four of my siblings, and my oldest sister who was in charge of all of us. It rained and rained. In the midst of all that drenching rain, we constantly had to hide from the government. Only one cow was giving milk, so the children got the milk and my elder sister and I survived on leaves. I stayed for almost three weeks, until the rain drove me back to Kuchdok.

I left the cattle camp carrying Atong in a goatskin sling and began the long trek back to Kuchdok. I didn't realize I was walking straight out of desperation and into death. Walking through the three villages along the road, I clung tightly to my baby as we passed the horror that lined the streets. The heavy air was filled with the stench of the dead and dying. I will never forget the sight of tiny babies still nursing on their dead mothers. My heart beat wildly with fear. I did not want to be one of the dead or dying. I kept repeating to myself, "I can't die like this."

How I made it through this period after Atong's birth is unclear to me: day to day, moment to moment, fighting waves of hunger. After we returned to Kuchdok from the cattle camp, water was scarce, and there was nothing to eat but apar, a kind of leaf that grows in the river. These leaves fed the people. We were hungry, but Atong was a healthy baby. As the situation grew increasingly grim in the village, many young mothers were dying. My cousin died after having a baby two months before me. I decided to leave. Many people were leaving, and I did not want to die. My uncle's brother-in-law, whom we knew as Uncle Gabriel, visited his sister in Kuchdok, and when he saw the situation there he came to find me and told me, "You have to leave now. Go to Ethiopia." I decided to leave immediately with my baby. When my mother learned that I intended to go, she sent one of my sisters, Adol, with me to help care for the baby. Adol was twelve or thirteen years old. My mother poured water on us as a blessing. We left her standing there still holding the water.

Walking to Ethiopia

Uncle Gabriel told me how to get to Ethiopia. He said to walk from Kuchdok to another small village called Marang, two miles away. There we would meet people who would show us the way to Anydie, another seven miles. At Anydie we would meet people who were going to Ethiopia. He also told me to walk only at nighttime so that we would not attract the attention of government soldiers.

When we got to Anydie, we found many people, and we hid in the trees for two days without food. There were some women who had food, but it was impolite to ask them to share. One man noticed we had no food, so on the third day, he gave my sister some flour.

My father's cousin, my Uncle Kuol (son of Ayak), came with his youngest daughter, Bok, four years old, and told me I must take her, or she would die. Another woman came with a five-year-old girl named Kuie and said, "You must take her to her mother in the next village." It turned out that Kuie's mother was already in Ethiopia, so that task was more difficult than I expected. I was now responsible for three little girls and a baby. When the choice came between myself and another young life, I knew I still must take her. Death was all around me; I had to take the chance on how we all would die. Bok is still with me today.

After three days at Anydie we moved on toward Ethiopia. We traveled with a group of maybe seventy people: men, women, and children. We became family. We walked for nine days across a large desert. Then our food gave out. We found a clearing in a wooded area and sat to wait, surrounded by the sounds of gunfire. Some men with our group went ahead to scout for a better place. Some would come back and report that soldiers were nearby, so we stayed where we were for safety.

After six or seven days, Atong became ill with dysentery from the flies and from being bumped around all the time. We decided to move on, walking at night because airplanes were flying overhead searching for people. During the day we hid among the trees, waiting for the cover of night. It took us one month to get to Ethiopia. We left in May and got there in June. People were sick, and one lady died. Our stomachs had shrunk so much that we could no longer digest food.

Chapter 3: Ethiopia

We learned we were in Ethiopia when we were stopped by a group of men who appeared from the jungle with guns and flashlights. They spoke to us in Arabic and frightened us, but we soon realized that they were Sudanese rebels. They greeted us warmly, told us we had reached Ethiopia, and gave us food. They told us that the next village would be Ethiopian and that there we would meet other people like them, who would help us with transportation to the UN camp known as Iteng. We spent the night at that Ethiopian village, and leaders of Ethiopian soldiers helped us get to the camp.

Iteng, UN Camp in Ethiopia

When we arrived at Iteng, people came out of the camp to check on the news from the villages. I was surprised to learn that my brother Thon was in the camp. He did not recognize me, because I was skin and bones. I cried when I saw him. He grabbed Bok, his niece, and prayed over her. He told me my husband was there. I was numb to the news.

My brother took Atong, and I held the other two children's hands, and we went to get ration cards. On the way home I ran into my husband Akech. He was curious to know whether our baby was a boy or a girl. He asked so many questions.

Akech was very shocked about how skinny I was. Thon was embarrassed about my condition, because it reflected poorly on our family. He told my husband that I was to go with him, Thon, until I was restored to a healthier condition. Also, this was still the period after the birth of a baby when the mother and baby customarily live with her family. He took me to the home of our cousin Jok where he was living. Jok had been killed in the war, but his wife, Nyankot, and her two-year-old were living there. I still had Kuie. I told Thon and Nyankot to look for Kuie's mother in the camp. They found her several days later. When Kuie's mother came for her, Kuie did not remember her and was shy and sad about leaving me. Her mother was joyful to have her daughter back, but Kuie and I parted sadly.

Soon after Kuie left with her mother, Bok became sick with measles. It started with a bad cough, and soon she had a high fever, watering eyes, and runny nose. She wouldn't eat. My neighbor came and said, "This is the measles. Put her in a net and cover her with a blanket." So I did that. Next day, she couldn't get up. The fever was very high.

The next day my sister came and said, "You are doing everything wrong. She is too hot; you will make her blind. We need to put her in water." We covered her in water and it looked like steam was coming out of her body. She felt better. Then the spots started to appear. We were so happy, because the spots were the sign of healing.

This was the summer of 1986. I stayed there for two months and became very healthy. I was safe in that camp, and there was a lot of food, but people still died of disease. Akech lived with a group of single men in a house that had no wife. They were waiting to train for the SPLA. Only three young boys were doing the cooking. I started taking them food every morning and evening. Akech could not eat the food, however, because the Alokthok ceremony had not been performed. Before we could be together, he was supposed to receive Alokthok from my parents. Therefore, I told Thon and Nyankot that I needed to move there to take care of Akech, and I moved out with their blessing. I showed up at the house where Akech was living with three children and a lot of dishes and household items given to me by the women I knew. We lived for three months in the single men's house and then began to build our own hut.

Akech and I made a home in this refugee camp. Our daughter Aduot (named after my husband's grandmother) was born on April 7, 1988. We all commented that she was a very lucky baby, because our ration came on that day, a day early. Rations came every fifteen days, but everyone would run out of food before the end of the ration period. The day Aduot was born, we all had food to eat before we expected it. And, importantly for a household where a baby had just been born, the ration included bar soap!

In 1988, there was a problem in Kuchdok, my old village. Because so many dead human bodies were lying around, the hyenas got a taste for human flesh. They became brave and ventured into the villages, killing children and even older people in their homes. My mother escaped to Iteng with my brother Mareach (six years old) and my sister Nyaluak (eight years old). My father had died, and she had promised him that she would bring the children to me. She left them with me and went back to Bor to be by my father's grave.

Now I had five children in my care: Adol, Atong, Bok, Mareach, and Nyaluok. My husband loved them all. My youngest brother, Mareach, was very funny. He was fascinated with newborn Aduot's hands, because her fists had not yet opened. He kept asking to see what she was holding in her hand. (It was he who had begun calling my baby Atong, *Child of the War*, and the name had stuck.) We all slept in one hut. Mareach would get up very early to play and would come back later to wake us up. He would say he just came from another village.

The girls were all enthusiastic about learning to cook. Bok was a very good cook at the age of nine. Everyone had a job in our full house. They were all good responsible children. We were happy. Our son Kut was born on December 7, 1989. He was a good healthy baby. My husband was very happy when he found out he had a son. He tried to help me cook, but I was too embarrassed to let him help. The children were good at taking care of the baby. Each of the older children took care of a younger child.

Bok and Mareach would always ask other villagers what they called things in their language, until they found out some words sounded like bad words in our language.

Bok learned languages really fast. She was often a translator, and she was the one I could send to the store. Mareach, wanted to learn every language. They were so helpful. They would learn the language of any tribe very fast. They don't remember any of them now.

Atong was very sweet and helpful. She played and sang like a grown girl. She had a good voice. She was shy, but not afraid. She never fought or yelled back. She was in charge of blowing the flames to get the fire started. That was her job. She knew how to make tea and wash dishes.

Aduot was the opposite of Atong. She talked a lot. "Baba" (father), she would say, "I want to kiss you." She was always asking me questions: "Why is your stomach so big? How did you get that baby in your stomach?" She was always in my lap. People would say, "Why are you sitting in your mom's lap? You are too big." When I had the baby she was glued to the baby and me. Sometimes she would drink the baby's milk and then say, "No, I didn't." She loved to tell on the other children. She did not like it if I dressed her like a boy. When I lost her, it was very bad; no one talked anymore.

We created a home in that refugee camp with three huts, a garden and animals for food. The UN supplemented our garden produce with staples like flour. Life was good except for the diseases.

Panicked Exodus from Iteng Camp

In May 1991 I was four months pregnant with our son Jok. A civil war had broken out in Ethiopia. We were hearing about it on the radio, but we did not expect it to displace us until we began to hear the sounds of gunfire on the other side of a distant mountain.

My husband's cousin Bior, the head of our family, came to our home one night and told us that we should prepare for a sudden evacuation. In that case, we should take the children to his place so that they could be evacuated in an orderly way with men to carry each of them.

The next morning when I awoke, people were streaming past the camp along the road to Sudan. A car went past with an amplified voice telling everyone to leave at once and go to Juko, a village in Sudan near the Ethiopian border. At seven o'clock that morning, I took the children to Bior's place and went home to prepare the goats to travel. At nine o'clock our camp manager drove through the camp announcing that everyone must leave because it was no longer safe there. "Pack your stuff and leave," he said. We prepared to flee back across the Sudanese border to a village of the Nuer people. My husband would have to stay behind to try to protect us.

We did not know we were leaving forever. We thought we'd be back that evening. We wanted to take our goats. Bior's sister Athew and I put our goats together and we put ten-year-old Mareach and her fourteen-year-old son, young Bior, in charge of them. They left before we did.

I prepared food and gathered blankets and cooking utensils and locked them in a hut so that they would be there when we came back. My aunt was there (my mother's cousin), an older lady, who often came to help me with the children. She came to help me prepare my household to leave. Suddenly we heard the sounds of gunfire. I told her not to go back to join her relatives, but she wanted to go to them. We argued, but she took off to find her relatives. I tied together small portions of food—corn, beans, sugar, flour, cooking oil—and carried them on my head and left to join my children at Bior's house.

Everyone except two-and-a-half-year-old Aduot had left my sister-in-law's house, so I left that house carrying Aduot and the food on my head. When I grew too tired to carry the food on my head, I went under the gate of an empty house to hide. My brother Garang saw me go under the gate, so he joined us and took Aduot and led me onto the road. He was running. There were thousands of people running too, and soon I lost my brother and Aduot. I was just running down the road among thousands of panicked people. There was screaming and chaos as everyone scrambled for their lives. The sounds of gunfire filled the air as we all ran blindly to find safety.

After about an hour I found eight-year-old Bok. I told her to stay with me, but it was easy to lose a child under those circumstances. The trail was narrow and lined with tall grass, but many people would leave the path and create separate trails. Bok would wander off onto one of those new trails. I could not turn around to see her because of the burden on my head. People would come between us. I kept calling her name and she would answer, but sometimes we would become separated. Then I would find her again.

Bok was with me all day, until the end when I lost her. When we finally stopped to regroup, I realized that Bok was not in sight. I was dizzy with panic. I grabbed everyone around me asking them if they had seen my child. I was crying and screaming, but everyone was too nervous and scared to help. I ran among the thousands and thousands of exhausted people, begging someone to help me, but everyone was filled with their own troubles. I looked to the sky and begged the Lord to help me.

A man came to me and said, "Quit standing there. You will get killed. You must move! Maybe she is ahead."

Praying that she was still alive, I made my feet move forward. I still had the bundle of food on my head. This was my lifeline, and I was not going to let it go.

We came to a small branch of the Nile River. I was very scared to cross the river with my huge, pregnant belly. I knew that the river bed had many deep holes made by footsteps of elephants that crossed before us. Many people became trapped in those holes and drowned. I entered the water carefully. My feet skimmed along the bottom, my toes searching for dangers. My hands were clinging tightly to the bundle on my head. Gingerly I moved ahead. Each step was for my daughter. Each step was away from the noise of the guns and the terror of certain death. The fear filled me and made my head swim with thoughts of my daughter.

I missed a step and plunged into a hole. I sank quickly to my neck, but I still clung to the bundle on my head. I was trapped by nature, my unborn child, and the precious bundle on my head. I watched in despair as children drowned around me, and a sick man gave up his life to the river's force. I looked for my brother who was carrying my baby and for the other relatives that I had entrusted with my children's lives. The guns were blaring in the background like a curse from a thousand demons. Everyone was running from an unnatural death that had sadly become a part of our lives. Reality had become so dark, it blocked out the African sun. I prayed.

I witnessed the horror of the battle between nature, man, and raw evil. Still I clung to the hope that I would be chosen to live that day. People were splashing water in my face as they made their way across the river. Finally four men, strangers to me, came to my rescue and pulled me out. My leg was swollen, but I managed to limp to the other side.

This other side of the river rang with a different sound of anguish. Thousands and thousands of people were calling out for their loved ones. The air rang with calls in many languages: Dinka, Nuer, Anyuak, Chuluk, Mendary… The shore was filled with sounds of panic and uncertainty. The wailing rose and filled the night. I couldn't find one person in my family. My leg was swollen and my voice joined the chorus of despair. I prayed and cried all night. The darkness held our fears close, and we waited for the dawn to bring hope.

In the morning everyone began frantically looking for family. Time was not on our side, and the urge to keep moving kept hovering like a pesky mosquito. I was frantic with worry about Atong and Kut. I assumed that my brother Garang had made it across the river with Aduot. Suddenly I recognized my cousin Auwr. She was looking for her children. She told me that Atong was with her and her husband. They had found her running alone on the road. She had also seen Kut; he was still with my sister-in-law. So I knew that Atong and Kut had made it safely to this side of the river.

Auwr went her way, and I went on searching for Garang and Aduot. Instead, I found my brother Mareach, still carrying the goat kid. He had lost all the other goats but clung to the baby goat, even when he was told to put it down and run. Neither he nor the goat had eaten in two days, but he still insisted on carrying it. Next I found Bok. She was the only child that had not thrown away her burden. She still had our cooking utensils. We were still missing Aduot. Finding her was very difficult.

I ran into Auwr again and learned from her that my relatives had gathered under a certain tree. I found them there: my uncle Kuol; his wife, whom we called Mom; my cousins Abeny, Ayak, and Achewel, and their children; and three of my nephews. My Aduot and my brother Durang were with them. I now had all my children, but I was still missing my sister Nyanluak. She was eight or nine years old then, and I was still responsible for her.

My uncle knew I was pregnant and exhausted, so he insisted that I sit down and rest. I sat down and looked around and realized that I was the only member of our family group who was carrying any food. I got back up, found firewood, and began to cook. I was so worried about Nyanluak that I could not eat. My mother would never have forgiven me if I had lost her. My uncle assured me that we would find her.

That night it rained really, really hard. We had no shelter, so we stayed awake all night. A woman gave birth to twins that night. Two women were helping her, and I went to help. They needed a fire to help them see, so I tried to bring fire, but the rain kept putting it out. We had to wait for lightning flashes to see to deliver the placenta and cut the umbilical cord. We worked fast during each bolt of lightning and then waited in the dark for the next bolt. We were expecting her to deliver the placenta, but a flash of lightning revealed a second baby's head! After both babies and their single placenta were delivered, we used a sharp blade of dry grass to cut the umbilical cord as our forebears used to do.

The morning of the third day, we were very wet, so our uncle directed us to lay out our bedding and clothes to dry. The ground all around was made bright and colorful with refugees' drying fabric belongings. Somebody stole my blanket while it was laid out to dry. Theft was a big problem throughout my refugee experience. My uncle's wife, Mom, gave me another one. Sometime later it was stolen while I washed it at the river; I just hung it on a tree to dry, went into the water to swim, and dipped my head in the water. And when I looked for it, it was gone.

I complained to my friend, and she said, "You are talking about a blanket? I brought a bar of soap. I have cared for it all this time. A goat just ate it!"

My cousin cut her blanket in half and gave one of the pieces to me.

On the third day, while we waited for our blankets and clothes to dry, Nyanluak joined us. She had gotten separated from my sister-in-law's group and had traveled with my cousin's brother-in-law. My Uncle Kuol's daughter was married to this man's brother. This man had recognized Nyanluak and taken her with his group. This group had been beset by a swarm of bees. When I found her, I could hardly recognize her swollen face.

By this third day, Nuer people from the nearest village had started killing and robbing refugees. Not all the Nuer villagers were hostile to us; friendly Nuer were advising us about the safest course of action. The elders among us met and decided we should all walk ahead to the next village.

Reunited with my family, we began to walk. Before long, I spotted three of my lost goats in the possession of two men. They demanded money for them, which my uncle paid. Now I had these three and the goat kid that Mareach had preserved: four of the thirty goats I had sent away with Mareach and Bior as we were leaving Iteng.

Our bodies were sore, and without the hope of survival we would all die of despair. We gathered up our pains and grief ready to face a brighter day. As we trudged on, men that were behind us caught up and shared their knowledge of what had happened back there. Some of these men were badly injured. I could see in their eyes that nobody else had survived. All the women asked about their husbands. The men sadly informed us that all the men who had stayed behind to defend us were dead. We insisted they confirm to us that our husbands could still be alive. They knew that what we hoped could not be true. All were dead and the bad was still coming.

I needed to grieve for my husband. He was a lovely husband and a lovely father. He was everything to me, my children and our people. No one was left alive. Unbelievable. There was no time to grieve properly, however.

We kept going until we came to a fork in the road. The grass was so high we didn't know which way to go. Some of us accidentally took the wrong branch. I was with my cousin Achwil and her children. With me were my son Kut, my sisters Bok and Nyanluak, and my brother Mareach. My daughters Aduot and Atong were with my uncle and our other relatives who had taken the main road. Our trail led to a big river. Some of the men went into the river to test its depth, and they quickly sank to their eyes. We could not cross there with the children, so we turned upriver, walking along the bank in high grass and deep mud, creating our own path.

The mosquitoes were terrible here beside the river. Many wild animals were concealed in the grass. Some of our people fell prey to animals along the trail. We passed the corpse of a woman relative of my husband. She lay beside the path, partially eaten, we could not tell by what—a hyena perhaps. We walked for eight hours in despair. Sometime after midnight, terrified of the wild animals, we stopped where a group of people had built fires, but there was no room for us to lie down there. We sat all night and did not sleep. At daylight, we began walking again. We walked all day, still in terrible conditions.

Around six in the evening, we came to a village called Pakada, where we were reunited with the people who had taken the good fork, the main road. I had feared that Aduot and Atong had suffered the same hardships as we had, so I was overjoyed to find them well. Imagine my surprise when they told me that their journey had been much easier than ours. We had simply taken the wrong route.

We spent the night in the village, finally getting some sleep. The next morning we were back on the road, heading for Pinchala (Pochalla), a village in southern Sudan on the Ethiopian Border. On the road, one of the goats became lame. I did not want the men to kill her, but allowed them to do so for food. Now we were down to two goats. I sold one for corn. The other was pregnant, so I could not kill her.

The children all knew how to set up a camp. I was very slow because I was pregnant. The children would run ahead to find us a good tree to camp under. Each child had a job: one would gather firewood, another would dig the hole for the fire, and others would set up camp. Then Nyanluak would run back to find me. I was the only adult, but the children were helpful and good.

We were on the road from Iteng to Pinchala from May to July. Every step, I wondered about my husband and grieved. There was nothing left but to stumble forward. Death was at our heels and we soon discovered it also thickly draped our destination. This became the walk of darkness. Our spirits were broken and we were all very hungry. Our own lives became war. We battled nature. Animals were eating our numbers and the mosquitoes fought for our thin blood. We could not fight back. God had abandoned us and seemed to be throwing us all away. Everything was trying to kill us. Why did we still live?

Chapter 4: Back to Sudan

We finally reached the border between Sudan and Ethiopia near the village of Pinchala. The Gilo River forms the international boundary there. Here we saw the Lost Boys. At that time they were known as the Red Army. We also called them *minors* at that time, because UN workers were using that term for them. They were very young. I asked one to help me carry my son. He helped me clear a space under a tree. I tried to cook a little food.

Crossing the Gilo River: Ethiopian-Sudanese Boundary

In the morning we had to cross the Gilo River, because, once again, we heard the sounds of guns behind us. Long lines of people were waiting at the river to get on boats. There were not enough boats. We waited in that line for a week. There were some men who were towing small children across the river in plastic sheets. I finally handed my children over to be placed in the sheets. My heart beat loudly as I watched my children cross the river. I was too pregnant to swim, so once again I was stuck. I waited two nights. All of us remaining on the shore could hear the approach of the guns. I was frightened for my children and I was frightened for myself. Finally four men from my husband's family came back to help me. They pulled me through the swift current. I was thankful they had not abandoned me. Thousands of people did not make it across the river. Government soldiers caught up with them there and massacred them.

My cousin Abeny met me on the other side. She told me that the village ahead had been stripped bare. The villagers were starving and even all the leaves had been eaten off the trees. People were coming back from that village with the news that people were dying of hunger there. The sounds of guns behind us gave us no choice. We wavered for a moment, but we decided to walk toward the hunger. This was not to be our day to die. We walked in the hot sun with no food or water: Abeny and I and our children. Because I was eight months pregnant, I was very slow, and one of the goats was limping badly. I finally convinced Abeny to go on ahead with her children and I would hide with mine. Bok and Mareach went ahead with Abeny; and Nyaluak, Kut, Atong, and Aduot stayed with me. My feet were badly swollen, and I could no longer walk. We hid in the jungle near the path for two days. Many people passed by us coming from the river. Many of them urged us to keep moving or we would die there.

We were all terribly thirsty. I knew I must go down to the river and find something for us to drink. We had been drinking dirty water along the way. Whenever we saw water on the ground we had scooped it up and trickled it down our swollen throats. I knew it was very bad for the children, but I had no choice. I went down to the river by myself.

When I reached the bank of the river, all was calm. But when I looked into the water I saw a dead body floating down in the current. I watched in horror as the river filled with bodies of people being massacred on the other side of the river. They floated past me, face down. For an instant all I could think about was my husband. I plunged into the river and tried to flip a body over. I was looking for the face of my husband. I began my desperate search. I kept flipping bodies over, but there were too many. I was weak from hunger, grief, and pregnancy. I could not keep up with the number of dead. I tried and tried to go on, but it was too much for me. I sank to the river bank and cried. My tears were for all the dead, all those left living, and my pain. I cried for what I didn't understand. I looked at the wasted lives flowing down the river, and I wondered who could save us.

I was weak from grief, but I remembered the lives of those living. I struggled to my feet and pushed the bodies back into the river. While the bodies silently floated by, I filled my container with water. My life had left me no choice. I went back to my children.

In my heart I now knew my husband was dead. The weight of this responsibility filled me up, but I did not have the luxury of despair. My immediate problem was getting food to my children. I knew if the children could make it until this baby was born, I could provide them all with food from my breasts. The idea formed in my head, until it became my survival plan.

After my encounter at the river, I knew I had to keep moving with my children. There was no going back now. Behind us there was no mercy. At least moving forward we had hope.

The lame goat died on the second day. One of my husband's relatives was there, and he skinned and butchered her for us. We shared the meat with all the people resting there near us in the jungle. I gave the skin to the first lady who asked for it. She needed it to carry her baby in. Then we started walking again toward Pinchala.

Two badly injured men crossed onto our path. I felt bad for their injuries, but I was desperate for news of my husband. I frantically asked them if they knew about some of the men behind them. Their flat reply was that everyone was dead. Their eyes told me the truth. I fell to my knees and looking up at the sky, I asked God what was happening. Why were we suffering? His answer was drowned out by the sound of approaching death. But the men's words I heard. "Move on!" My sorrow would have to wait another day.

We kept hearing the rumors that the village ahead was dying of starvation and that even the leaves had been eaten from the trees. We smelled the scent of death as we approached our destination.

Pinchala

In Pinchala we found animals and people lying everywhere, suffering and waiting for a death that was too slow to come. We stayed there for a month, intending to move on as soon as we could to my home village of Bor where my mom was. It was the rainy season, and we had to wait for the rivers between Pinchala and Bor to go down. Men would walk to the rivers to check on the water and return to tell us that it was still unsafe to cross. Eventually we realized we would have to spend the entire rainy season there in Pinchala. I was very pregnant and very sick.

Two problems we faced were biting flies and mosquitoes. The flies would come during the day and cover our children's faces. The children were so weak they didn't have the strength to swat the flies away. Their big eyes would follow us as they quietly waited to die. About 5:00 every evening the mosquitoes would swarm in, carrying malaria and inflicting more misery.

The Red Cross gave us a little salt after we complained that we needed it. We were so excited on the day that the salt was coming. We ran to the ration place and stood in line for a long time. Each family got a tablespoonful. I put ours in a small bag and tied it very tightly. I reached into a small hole in a tree and placed the precious salt there. Later I saw the children licking their hands. I did not know what they were doing. When I went to the tree to get the salt for cooking it was gone. All the children had found their parents' salt and had eaten it. Even the babies had held out their hands and shared in it. When I left for America, I promised the women I would send them back some salt. But I had no way to communicate with them, so I never sent any. People were always leaving, but no one was going back. It was a one-way trip.

Pinchala is a village of Anyuak people. They were really mean. We had to sell our best dresses to them to get corn. If we told them, "That is not enough corn for this beautiful dress," they replied, "Then go and eat your dress." They would not let us use their mortars and pestles to make flour from the corn. They hid the pestles from us. When it rained, we would take shelter with our babies under the eaves of their huts. They turned their dogs out of their huts to drive us away. They had an infestation of some kind of boring bug that got under our skin. We carried those bugs until we got to Kapoeta.

So we stayed in Pinchala and waited for help. As a group we began to pray. We knew God was the only one who could help us. We prayed very hard for him to forgive us and lend us his help. We knew that what was happening to us was not our fault. We felt like the new children of Israel. Like them, we were driven from our home, and we just wanted to follow Jesus. Flies, mosquitoes, snakes, and scorpions all wanted our blood, but our hearts belonged to Jesus. We knew all this misery was not our fault, but we still prayed for forgiveness and Jesus' mercy. We were pushed from our homes, but we had no Moses to guide us.

The worst of this bleak journey was how helpless we were to save our own children. We devised many plans to care for the children. At night when the mosquitoes came, one adult would swat them away while we quickly tried to cover six children with one net. They would huddle together under the net trying to arrange themselves into a fitted puzzle so they could sleep. Then the adults would build a fire and sit around talking deep into the night. We tried to plan and find a solution to our problems. We would have great talks. Often other adults would shoo the mosquitoes away while I got under the net because I was pregnant, and they wanted to help me avoid disease.

When the goat kid was born, Mareach took it to the mosquito net. The children fought for the middle of the net to escape the mosquitoes. The baby goat figured out how to run and get to the net first. One night people came and stole the mother goat, so I had to take her kid to the cattle camp that the refugees in Pinchala had set up. Mareach would go visit him every day and come back with updates. I had some cows in that cattle camp that my husband's cousin's husband had been caring for ever since we left Iteng. (Sometime later, he would be killed in a raid on the herd by an enemy tribe.)

I would pray and sing this song to the children: "Halaluya ana mashi le bet a buie/Halaluya halaluya ana mashe le bet a buie" (Halleluah, I'm going to my Father's house). The language of this song is local Arabic (or *Juba Arabic*), the spoken Arabic of Africans in South Sudan, especially in and around Juba.

I would sing this song every night to my children. This was a nightly relationship check between me and my God. At this time Aduot became very sick. My tears fell like rain. I was battling Death everyday, and he was trying to find my family in the darkness.

The United Nations would bring us a little food. They would fly overhead and drop bags of beans. Many people were so anxious for the food they would run toward the sound of the planes. Some were killed by the falling food. The bags contained beans that were hard like little rocks. We had none of our cooking supplies, so we had to chew the beans to soften them. When the beans were a little softer we would feed them to the children.

My little girl was so sick it was hard to get her to swallow food. In order to save her, I volunteered to work in a hospital. Unfortunately, the hospital was in another village. I begged the Sudanese Red Cross volunteers to put me on the list to go. The airplanes that brought Red Cross food could only take two or three people, twice a day. Every morning for about nine days I walked to the river where the list was posted on a tree. This was a very stressful time because not only was my baby very sick, but I was getting very close to giving birth. I did not want to have my baby here in this valley of death.

One morning I found my name on the list. I was so happy, but I knew I would have to leave my little siblings, Mareach (age seven) and Nyaluak (age ten), with my cousins Abeny and Ayak. Only my name and those of my children were on the list. I was able to smuggle Bok onto the plane by having her carry Aduot. Mareach and Nyaluak were devastated and scared. We counted on each other for support and survival. We all cried very hard as we boarded that plane. I kept promising my siblings that we would be together again soon. I heard the cries of Mareach and Nyaluak long after the airplane left the ground. I stared ahead to the future so my heart would not be broken from the past. I had to help my daughter.

Village of Narus, 1991

We flew across the Kenyan border into the area called Lokichogio, known as Loki. I couldn't understand the pilot when I asked him where we were going. All I could make out was that when we landed a truck would take us back into southern Sudan to the town of Kapoeta. On the plane we were given no food, so we were excited when we finally landed. Eager to get on with our journey, we tumbled off the plane looking for the truck that would take us to the hospital. There was no truck.

A Dinka woman had flown in with us on the plane. We became instant relatives. Her name was Nyanror. She stayed with us until we reached Kapoeta, and I have not seen her or heard of her since. Soon after we arrived in Loki I left her with the children and went for water. When I came back, we cooked and ate dinner and felt better.

We were expecting Mareach to follow us on the next plane out of Pinchala, but he had not arrived. I was very worried. At long last a truck came, driven by a Kenyan. He and his Kenyan companion gestured to us to get into the truck, so we did. The truck was carrying about twenty refugees from Pinchala. I was very, very worried about Mareach, but if we did not go with this truck there might never be another one. As we drove away, I sat in the truck worrying about Mareach.

After awhile our driver pulled over to the side of the road. Both Kenyans got out and began to fight each other. Everyone else on the truck was watching and wondering about the fight, but I was still worrying about Mareach. I saw a plane fly overhead and thought perhaps Mareach was on it. The fight went on and on until another truck drove up. I stood up and a man in the second truck recognized me and called out my name. When I looked over, he held up Mareach and passed him over to helping hands in our truck. Mareach had indeed been on the plane that I saw. That second truck's driver stopped the fight and our driver got back behind the wheel and our trip continued.

We arrived at night in Narus. I sat my children by the side of the road. Nyanror stayed with them while I went to see if I knew anyone in the village. As luck would have it, I found a hut that housed a few women I used to know. I asked for food for my children. They did not have food to spare, but they did give me some of what they had. I quickly returned to my children and found them all asleep on the side of the road. In this new place there were no mosquitoes or biting flies. They would awake from nightmares of being bitten, but we would joke that it was just a dream. People often ask me if my children whined or complained about their extreme suffering. Even when there was no food for days my children did not cry. They were good children with amazing strength. They seemed to sense that I was trying as hard as I could to keep them alive.

This village had a three-sided hut where my little family could stay until a truck could get through the weather. We waited each day, but there was much rain, so no truck could come. I lived in fear that my little hut would collapse and hurt my children. Why was there always a problem ahead of me? There was so much pain and suffering surrounding me that I knew even God was overwhelmed. No one cares about other people when they are so busy helping themselves. Therefore it was very strange when a man offered me one of his huts. I quickly went inside and cleaned out our new home. This would be a place to stay at least until the rain stopped. I had no one to tell, but it was getting very close to the time my baby would be arriving. I was very sick, and I was having problems passing urine. I knew I needed a hospital.

The man who had given me his hut was very concerned about me. He kept telling me that as soon as transportation arrived I must go. My children's lives depended on my survival. I was feeding my children leaves, and my baby daughter was very sick, but I knew if she got real food she would survive. I waited ten days until a truck finally came. We still couldn't leave because of the weather. After twenty-one days we left. The trip took two days. We had no food on the truck. The driver was from Nairobi. He had a little food that looked like cakes. They were very sweet. My children hadn't had food for so long, they had forgotten how it tasted. Their little faces puckered as they tried to eat the cake.

Kapoeta

We reached Kapoeta in the afternoon. It used to be a town, but it had burned down. I felt happy to be back in Sudan until I saw the depth of the destruction. Everything looked bad. The buildings were burned and deserted. I cried. I had such high hopes for this place. This was supposed to be the light at the end of the tunnel. Instead it was another path full of rocks that I must stumble across.

The Red Cross would leave arriving refugees on an old soccer field shaded by a single large tree. I gathered up my children and tucked them in under that tree until I could find someone to help us. We did not know anyone in Kapoeta, so we waited there. News of new arrivals would spread through the refugee community in Kapoeta, so people would come to see whether they had relatives there. After about an hour, a very skinny woman walked in front of us, and I recognized her as my cousin Amej.

I was very happy to see someone I knew. I quickly told her of my travels and my need to get to the hospital. She said it was very unlucky that I came back, because life at this place was very bad. I noticed she was wearing a black dress. She said her husband had been killed and she was trying to keep her own two children alive. Her hut was full because there were two other families living there, but she told me to come along with her. We walked into her bare little home. There were no blankets or any extras to ease my children's pain. I put down a shirt and they all huddled together on it. I had thought I was coming to a better place, but this was much worse.

My cousin explained how life had changed here. There were five huts, and each hut had a big hole behind it. Every day airplanes came to kill us. She told me that if I heard an airplane coming I was to tell the children to run and divide themselves among the holes. With everyone scattered that way we had a better chance that someone would survive.

I kept asking myself why I had come back here. As we walked through what was left of the village, I asked about the hospital and learned that it was only a small hut left by the UN and that it was a distance away. When I got back to my cousin's hut, a woman had given a small amount of food to my children. I watched them out playing in the mud. They were just skin and bones. I did not know how they even had the energy to play. I held my sick child on my lap. Two days later, on September 8, my contractions started.

I summoned my cousin and told her I must go to the hospital. She found me a boy—he was one of the Lost Boys—to help me get to the hospital. The Lost Boys were always such helpful boys. I prayed for them. This little one was eleven years old. He took me to the hospital. When we arrived, there were just three other ladies. We looked at each other. Who would help us? One of the ladies had a baby wrapped onto her back, but she didn't know much about delivering babies.

The hospital was a hut with a dirt floor and a grass roof. It had a wooden structure that a woman could hold onto while giving birth like an animal. I had no time; I was the first to get into the structure. There I gave birth to my beautiful baby boy. The ladies quickly took him and laid him on the ground.

We waited for the afterbirth to come out. It would not come out of my stomach. No one knew what to do. One of the women tried to pull it out, but my uterus came out with it. I lay back on the wooden bed, frustrated with my body. All my limbs started to swell. I lost consciousness. I had lost a lot of blood. I lay there from nine o'clock that night until six the next morning. All around me I could hear the women talking, saying that I was dead. I could hear, but I could not move or speak.

They sent the watchman with a message to a woman in another village. She came on a bicycle to help me. When she arrived everyone thought it was too late because I was already dead, but she knew what to do. I don't know exactly what she did, but late in the morning I woke up. I asked about the baby. The women handed me a healthy, sweet baby boy.

They told me I must carry the baby back. I was too weak and I was still losing a lot of blood. There was no extra cloth to help me stop the flow of blood. I used my shirt to strap the baby onto my back and started walking slowly back to my family. On the way back I heard the airplanes coming. I don't know how I did it, but I ran. I found a hole near somebody's home and jumped into it with the people who lived there. I stayed there until I heard the sound of the planes fade away. When I got out of the hole and started walking toward home, I passed a crying woman. A plane had just killed all fourteen people in her family. A bomb had made a direct hit on the hole where they had taken shelter. I hurried on very afraid of what I would find. By some miracle my entire family had survived. I collapsed on the floor, overcome by fatigue and fear.

It took me seven days to recover enough to walk back to the hospital with my sick daughter. Fortunately there was a man there who was a doctor. He gave my sick baby medicine, a blanket, a bottle of oil, and some soap for the lice that infested us. These small tokens of comfort meant so much to me. After the despair and hopelessness, the hardest part of living in my situation was the lack of little comforts that most people take for granted. There was never a warm blanket to ease the pain of a chilly night, or a cup of hot tea to help soothe the loss of a family member. Little comforts that are naturally taken for granted when life is in balance are lost when the world is filled with the blankness of survival.

The doctor told me that Aduot needed medicine. With medicine it could still take eight months for her to get better. My head was racing with thoughts of how I could possibly stay there eight months longer with the lack of food and the deadly airplanes.

I wanted to run back to my own village, but it had been destroyed by people from the Nuer tribe, and many of my people had been killed. Intertribal fighting was also a threat where we were, because the government in Sudan encouraged fighting among the tribes. With tribes fighting each other, the government was free to be corrupt and to control its weakening people.

One day during this period I was traveling along a road with my baby. I had to take shelter in the trees with a group of strangers to escape an ambush. My baby was crying and I could not make him quiet. I could see in the strangers' eyes that they wanted me to do whatever I had to do to silence him. One woman said, "You need to keep that baby quiet." I told her I was doing all I could. The baby kept crying, and gunfire continued.

Another woman said, "You need to do something about that baby." I didn't get her meaning.

Then a man said, "Do you want us all to die here?"

Finally, I understood. They were not saying directly what they wanted me to do, but I could see it in their eyes. I stared back at them, and they knew that I would never do as they wanted. As soon as I could, I got away from those people. I was afraid of what they might do to my baby. I heard that a mother in another village had drowned her baby to keep it from giving away a large group of her relatives. People didn't want to talk about this kind of thing, and they still don't.

At this time my new baby was doing well. I was able to get my eighteen-month-old child to begin nursing again, but Aduot, who was four years old, would not nurse. I was very worried that she would not survive. I needed to be able to feed my children while we all waited for medical treatment to arrive. The medicine never came. The only thing that was constant was the sound of the killer airplanes that came every night. I knew I must get home to Bor to get help from my relatives. I was warned repeatedly not to go. As I was frantically planning what I should do, my brother Thon found me. He told me not to hold onto the hope that my husband was still alive. He said he knew where our mother was, and he would go find her. I was to stay put until he came back with news of my mother. After waiting one month for his return, I feared he too had been killed.

All this time I still prayed to God. I knew this situation was not God's fault, but it was very hard to understand. I also knew I didn't die because God was keeping me alive for a reason. I prayed for the life of my daughter, but many days went by without medicine.

One night in December she cried for food. My children were very good about not asking for food. I went around to my neighbors to beg for a little food to feed my daughter. In my heart I knew this was the end of my child's life. I blamed myself because I was her mother, and I was supposed to be able to care for my children. She began to have seizures and I could do nothing. My tiny daughter struggled between life and death for a whole day. I watched her suffer as my heart broke. I had no time to cry. The day she died was the saddest of my life, but I had no time to give in to my grief.

I knew I needed to bury my daughter, so I asked the help of my brothers-in-law. We had to bury her one mile away. It was very dangerous because the burial site was in another tribe's area. We went late at night and crept into the darkness as silent as a stalking lion. As we buried my small daughter, I wanted to die. My friend Debrah prayed for me, my husband, and my baby. She reminded me I was a daughter of God and a strong woman. The darkness surrounded me inside as well as outside. I wanted to give up.

The next day when she came to visit, I was sitting straight up. I still had three children to care for. If this is what the devil had planned for us, I would not give up.

We heard that the government was headed our way to kill everyone. We ran, this time closer to the border and all spread out. I decided to go toward Kenya for the water. Again I met up with the Lost Boys. It was strange that in the middle of nowhere I would run into those I knew. The boys again helped me. They carried the baby for me and gave me a little of their corn. They loved to play with my boys but scolded me if the boys pooped in their area. They were very funny.

Early in March, Nyaluak joined us. Pinchala had been overrun by government soldiers, and everyone there had run. Many were killed, and we were afraid Nyaluak had been among them, but she and my cousin Abeny survived and walked a long way until they were able to get onto a Red Cross truck that was taking Lost Boys to Kapoeta.

Leaving Kapoeta

Since we arrived in September 1991, I had been hearing rumors that the government's army would come and kill us. In March 1992, the rumors reached a peak. The SPLA had captured the area around Kapoeta, and the government wanted to take it back. Government soldiers could be expected to kill everyone in areas held by the SPLA.

Many of the people in the village thought that nothing was going to happen, but I knew in my heart that something would go wrong.

My cousin Amej was building her hut. I told her, "You don't need to build this hut; we will be leaving soon. I heard the rumor that the government is sending armies to come to this village and kill us."

My cousin told me, "No! Don't listen to those rumors. They are just rumors, and you don't need to worry about it. I need to build this hut, and maybe I will build another hut too." I said I didn't want to argue with her, but I was nervous. So I left her and went to my cousin Panchol. He was drunk as usual. I told him that I had heard rumors that armies were coming to the village to kill us. I told him we needed to leave and go somewhere else.

He said, "You know what? You are not on my neck." That is what he said. He said, "I will not carry you on my neck. Don't worry about anything. I am not worrying about anything." He did not understand what I was saying, so I left again.

I went next to the market to talk to one of my colleagues from the school. She had a rakuba, a small booth, there where she sold tea. I met her on the way and told her that I was hearing rumors about the disaster that was coming. I advised her to leave, but I didn't even know where to advise her to go.

But she was married at that time, and she had her family. And she told me, "You know what? You have been nervous too much. Don't be nervous. There is nothing that will happen. I will help you." She told me she would help me make some tea, and we could sell it in that market. In the hut there she was making tea and selling it to people in the market. She told me she would be working with me and helping me to make my own tea there and sell it so I could support my family.

I looked at her and said, "Oh, my goodness. What do these people think? I am looking at these people and telling them that there are rumors that this village will be destroyed in no time, and nobody is listening to me. What am I going to do?"

So I went home. I was just sitting there with my three siblings and my three children, and I was nursing my baby. I didn't know who else I could talk to, because whoever I talked to, they did not understand. My husband's cousin Wal stopped by the gate (compound) to visit. He was in the village to shop for a dowry because he was going to get married. He was a soldier in the SPLA, so I asked him about the rumors I was hearing. "Is it true?"

He told me, "Yes, that is true. So, if you have a place to go, you need to go with your children."

So I looked at the kids. I knew that one of the children had just died, and now I had three remaining. But it was hard for me to carry all three of them. I knew that Red Cross trucks were carrying Lost Boys away from the fighting to the border between Kenya and Sudan. They were using the old soccer field as a staging area. So I told the kids we needed to leave right away, and I started making food to take with us.

At the old soccer field, I talked to one of the guys who was in charge of the trucks. He told me no, there would be no room for other people. It was only for minors. I begged him to take us with him because I had heard rumors that the village would be destroyed. He told me no, and then he left. But I saw his family sitting by the truck. They made a line there with their stuff. So I went there and I put my small sack with a few clothes and our food in the line with that family. The man had two wives, and some of his relatives came and threw away my bag. I put it back in the line. When they saw that I would not do what they wanted me to do, they just left me there and went to a different place and made a new line. So I told my children that these people were not going to take us, and we needed to go to a different truck.

There were many more trucks in the area. So I went to a different truck. The sun was very, very hot. I put my stuff down and told the children to go under the tree and wait there. I was hoping there would be someone that I knew. I was lucky. I saw my cousin Mabior from Kuchdok. He was one of the men in charge of the Lost Boys. I asked him if they could take me with them in the truck, and he told me, "We don't know yet, because maybe the truck will be full. But you can wait here."

So I waited there with the children all day. The sun was very hot. When finally they loaded the truck, they let the minors onto the truck and it was nearly full. I was afraid that they were going to leave us behind.

I kept begging Mabior. I said, "The truck is getting full. Let me go in, please."

He kept saying, "Wait, wait, wait." It was noisy, and everyone was trying to get onto the truck and, there were lots of people and lots of Lost Boys. I kept begging him to please let me go in with my children because the truck was getting really full, and it would leave.

At the last moment, he said, "OK."

So I helped one of my siblings first. I threw one of my sisters and then my other sister into the truck. It was a long truck. I grabbed my younger brother and threw him in there. I put my siblings in first and the truck was about to leave. I was rushing, throwing the children into the truck, and when I started with my children I started with my daughter and then my son. And then I threw the baby in there. Luckily one of the Lost Boys caught him. He was seven months old. The truck was leaving—it was moving—and I put my hand on the top of the truck and I held it and put my one foot on the wheel, and the wheel was moving, and then I started to put my other foot up there too, and the truck was moving with me, and my hands were up there, and my children were in the truck. I was panicking, afraid I would not make it into the truck. Just in time, Mabior pushed my butt up there, and I fell on the children in the truck, and the truck was moving.

I found myself sitting inside the truck, and I looked to see where my baby was. One of the Lost Boys was holding him. There was no way for me to go and get him, because he was so far ahead in the truck and we were all crowded in so tightly. I started crawling between people and everyone was yelling at me that I was pushing and hurting them. I wasn't even listening. I was just going to my baby. I reached him and grabbed him as everyone was finding a place to sit. We were just sitting on top of each other because the truck was so full. Next I looked for my son Kut, who was two years old. I saw him crowded in among Lost Boys. I yelled at them, "Pick up that baby!" So one of them picked him up and held him. Next I spotted my daughter Atong. I sent Nyaluak crawling through the boys to get her. So then I had the baby, one of the Lost Boys was holding Kut, and Nyaluak had Atong. All my children were safe.

The truck was moving, and there were no good roads. The road was full of holes, so the truck was going very roughly and making lots of noise. It was going up and down, throwing us up and down in the truck. The ride was so bumpy that the boy who had Kut could not hold onto him. The boys passed Kut from one to another until he was back in my hands. We were in such a dangerous area that the truck would not stop, so everyone was peeing in the truck, and pee ran all over the floor. I had it all over me.

Narus Again

Somehow, we made it. We left Kapoeta around two o'clock in the afternoon. In the middle of night, we reached the village of Narus near the border with Kenya. Everybody got out of the truck and started to sweep the rocks away so we could lie down on the ground. None of us had blankets, so we lay down in the middle of nowhere in that village. In the morning the girls went for water and we cooked with the small amount of flour that I had brought. In the evening we didn't have anything else. The Lost Boys had corn that the Red Cross had given them. They gave us some and we cooked it and chewed on it all day.

The next day we tried to find a tree because it was so hot during the day. Narus was in the desert, and it was very hot with few trees. So I asked Bok, Nyaluak, and Mareach to go and find a tree for us so that we could sit in for the shade. We found a tree and shared it with some other people. In the evening, we would go back to that desert area so we could sleep there. We stayed in Narus for a couple of months and later we found out there was no going anywhere.

In Kapoeta we had been waiting to go to our own villages. I was planning to go back to Bor. Now, government soldiers had captured most of the other villages. I learned that Bor was under government control. I also learned that a week after we left Kapoeta, it was destroyed, and everyone was killed, including my colleague, the one who was telling me to make tea and support the family. Of her family, only one of her daughters, who was seven, lived. She reached Narus with her grandmother. I was crying, and I didn't want to tell the daughter that I had talked to the mother and told her that I wanted them to leave with me. My cousins in Kapoeta had run in time and reached the Ugandan border, but many people in Kapoeta were killed or lost in the desert. I felt lucky that God had pushed me and made me leave that village. I knew that everywhere I went, there was a problem there, and everywhere I left, I left a problem behind me.

After the two months in Narus, we decided we needed to build. That village was a desert. It was very hard to find grass and trees. To improve our housing situation, I decided to teach at a school for Lost Boys. They were housed in a compound of tents that had a school under the trees. I went there and applied to teach. I passed a test and became a teacher. After I was accepted, the United Nations gave us some things like tents, blankets, mosquito nets, seeds, and other things that I got for volunteering to teach. So I had a great tent, and we put it down and made a home.

Still there was no water. The water was a mile from our camp, so I would send my younger sisters to the water pump. The line there was so long that one or another of them would have to wait there all day before they could fill our three containers. They took turns holding our place in line. When finally our containers were filled, one of the girls had to wait there with our water while another came to get me. I would carry the water to our tent, one container at a time.

The water was the only problem we had there. The supply was so limited that we could use it only for cooking and drinking. We could not shower or wash with it. That was the way we lived.

Leaving Narus

In June 1991 the rumors came again that the government was sending armies to kill us. I was about to cook, and then these rumors came, and my sisters went to get water. A man was walking among the homes in the camp announcing it. He was saying, "Pack your stuff and go to the road that leads to Kenya." He was speaking softly so that the Taposa people living near us would not find out that we were leaving and tell the government army. Taposas had been cooperating with the government against the SPLA. The government was encouraging intertribal conflict.

I ran to the water pond to get my siblings. I told them, "Let's go now." So, we left in the evening, around seven o'clock. The road was full of people carrying children, carrying big loads, carrying sticks, bumping into each other at night. The children and I were going together, but when we finally got on the road, I couldn't see them anymore after three hours. I couldn't see my siblings. I was just with Atong and Jok. My brother Garang took two-year-old Kut and tied him on his back. Mareach, Nyanluak, and Bok made their own way without us, even separate from each other. They were experienced at this by now.

So we left and we walked and walked and walked. It was a lot of walking. Night turned to morning and we were still walking. Jok was on my back, and I was holding a container of oil. My cousin Abeny and I were both wearing white dresses, because we had learned that our husbands had died. While we lived in Narus, a man from my husband's family came to confirm that he was dead. That was my signal to begin the mourning customs. That is the way the culture is. If you become a widow, you wear a white dress for six months. After that, the husband's family will do prayers like a memorial, and then you will wear a black dress after that. I was wearing a white dress. It wasn't six months yet. My hair was shaved off. This is how the culture is. If your husband dies, your hair will be shaved off and you wear a white dress, and you will not put any beads or necklace on your neck or in your ears. You do not look good any more. You will just be a natural person. After six months, you wear the black dress and put a black scarf on your head, but still no necklace— no nothing. This is the way the culture is. After two years, they will do another memorial and then you can take off your black. You shave your head for a second time, but you can wear the necklace and earrings. That means the time of grieving is over. At that time, if you are still a young woman, your in-laws will sit down with you and ask you to choose one of your in-laws to become your new husband. But you don't call him your husband, you call him your in-law. Even if you have children with him, your children will call him *uncle* and not *father*, because that is the way the culture is.

While I was walking from Sudan to Kenya, I was wearing a white dress because I was grieving. So we walked and walked and walked and walked. One of the principals at the school had gotten me a huge container of oil, sixteen liters. At that time, everybody was hungry for oil. He told me the oil was for me to sell to help me with my children, or I could use it for cooking. It was up to me. I thanked him for that. He also got me a mosquito net and some clothes. He told me he knew my husband and he was very sorry. That was a very nice thing for him to do. I said to myself that I was going to keep the oil, and I was not going to use it. So the day we had to leave that village, I looked at the oil and wondered why I didn't just carry it with me. That way if I met some people who needed oil I could sell it to them for anything.

So the night we left, I put that oil on my head. It was very heavy, and I had to have someone help me get it on my head. I tied the baby on my back. We walked with thousands of people. I was holding my daughter's hand. One hand was holding the oil on my head, and the other was holding the hand of my baby. I didn't even have a hand to chase the flies from my face or scratch myself if I was itching. My two hands were full. My daughter was five years old. I walked two days and two nights, and everybody was passing me because I could not walk very fast. I had too much with the heavy oil, the baby on my back, and my daughter at my side. I saw lots of people passing me.

The third day we were very tired and very hungry. The baby was breast-feeding, so he wasn't as hungry. He didn't look hungry, but he was hungry at times. My daughter could not walk any more. She was very hungry and she was thirsty. We had no water, and we were in jungle. I decided to sit down under a tree by the side of the road. Atong lay down. I put her head on my lap and the baby on my lap too, and I was just sitting there in the middle of the jungle. Not very many people were walking. I think everybody had gone under the trees because it was so hot and everybody was tired and hungry and thirsty. I kept telling my daughter to hold on, because God would help us. I looked at her mouth and saw her tongue turning yellow because of the thirst. It was a very bad situation. We sat there until the sun cooled down a little bit, and I encouraged her to walk again with me.

The road was rocky, and we were walking between the hills. The border is in an area with lots of hills or mountains. The rocky road hurt my feet really bad. On that third day, my brother came with my son on his back and he met us there. We laughed at each other and we told my daughter to hang in there. He told me he was going ahead. I waved at my son Kut who was on his back. Kut was very hungry, but I didn't even look at that. I just waved at him.

Then I called Garang back again to ask if those were his boots on his head. He said they were. I asked if he was going to wear them. He said, "No, if I wear them they hurt my feet even more."

I asked if I could try them because my feet were killing me with the rocks. They were swollen. He gave me the boots and told me they were just going to hurt my feet. I said to just give them to me, and I took them from my brother. They were soldier boots. I put them on, and I thought they felt better. Oh, my goodness! I wore them all day. The next thing I knew, my feet were hurting really bad, but I didn't want to take them off. I would rather wear them than hurt my feet on the rocks.

That night we reached a place where a group of people were resting. We stopped to see whether supplies would arrive there. After an hour or two, the Red Cross came with trailers of water. Everybody started fighting to get some. I told my daughter to sit down with the baby while I went for our share. Red Cross workers were pouring the water into four or five barrels through a big hose. Everybody was trying to grab the hose to fill their containers with water. The Red Cross workers struggled to keep control of the hose and fill the barrels. I went into that mess and fought for ours. Water sprayed all over our heads, and we ran back and forth trying to grab the hose. People were leaning into the barrels to get water, and some were falling in.

I grabbed some water and went back and put water on my babies' heads. I knew that if I put it into their mouths, they would not swallow. My daughter's tongue was yellow, and her mouth was so dry. She couldn't even sit up anymore, so I held her head and put some water on it and on her ear. I had heard from others that when you are that thirsty you shouldn't drink at first. You put water on your body to cool it down before you drink. If you drink first, you will die. So I put water on her and did the same thing for the baby. Then, I put a little water in their mouths. Then I did the same for me. It hurt so bad to swallow that water, because of the swelling in my throat, and because my mouth was so dry. When I swallowed the water, tears came out of my eyes. The same thing happened to my daughter. After we rested a little bit, we decided to move again.

The next day we reached the border. All my relatives were there ahead of me. I was the last one to show up. There were sick people, old people, disabled people, and people who had babies on the way. Those were the people I came with. Some of my relatives had been there three days before us, but I could not go any faster because of my daughter. Some of my husband's relatives came back to look for me. They found me and told me I was close.

My husband's cousin Wal took my daughter. He said, "You are all going to die here. Let me help you." He took my daughter and put her on his neck. Then it was just my baby and me. Wal and my daughter got to the border a day and a half before me.

When I arrived there, I found my daughter. She was smiling. I sat down and she came running to me and told me all her stories about how she came there and they gave her some tea and she tried to swallow it, and she couldn't because her throat hurt so bad. She was telling me all her stories. She told me, "That will happen to you too now, Mama. When you drink the tea you will see, and you will cry." I was laughing, and I said that it would not happen. A relative got me some tea and told me to just do it—just do it. I grabbed the tea and tried to put it in my mouth, but I couldn't swallow it, and I spit it out. People were yelling at me that I needed to drink it so my throat would open. When I took a drink and swallowed a little bit, tears came out of my eyes. I started to sweat, and my daughter said, "See, I told you! This is what I went through."

Having reached the border, we started walking again. I took off my boots. Oh, my toes! My toenails came off in the boots. I didn't even feel it. Everyone was shocked that my nails came off.

Many people along the way had told me to throw away the cooking oil that I was carrying, because other people were throwing their things away when those things became too heavy. But I did not want to throw that oil away. I kept thinking about what would happen later, not what was happening then. I lost all the hair on the crown of my head because of carrying that oil. Whenever I put it down for a little rest, I became very light. I wanted it back, because it had become part of my balance. When I took it off, I felt dizzy, like I was going to fall down.

Chapter 5: Kenya

I reached Kenya in 1992 and stayed there until 1994. I had spent half my life wandering from danger to danger and hunger to hunger. When I finally reached safety I couldn't stop crying. Those were the tears of a widow. My eyes were raining with grief. I couldn't stop the flood of misery that my eyes had seen.

When I first reached Kenya, my baby, Jok, was very sick. He was six or seven months old. I was afraid that he would die. We would sing and pray around him. The UN had a small hospital there in a big tent, so I took him to it every day, and they gave us Pedialyte. That was all we got. All my children suffered from malnutrition, and the UN hospital gave them Pedialyte and provided tubs of water where we mothers could put our children to keep them cool. UN workers encouraged us to alternate breast-feeding with Pedialyte. Like many mothers and their children, we spent our days there in the tent and went home at night. We lived beneath a big tree. The shade of the trees we called shadows. We refugees shared the shadows with each other.

We stayed in Loki for a couple of months just inside the border between Kenya and southern Sudan. UN workers wanted us to move farther from the border to Kakuma Refugee Camp, where we would be safer. Kakuma was a new camp, so we had to wait for them to survey a town site for us. When I asked a UN worker when we could go to Kakuma, he told me we were still waiting in Loki because the UN had not yet found a place to put the cemetery for refugees.

Kakuma

When finally we moved to Kakuma, we camped in the middle of nowhere under the trees. It was a desert. Our legs would sink into the dust to our knees. The babies would try to crawl, and the dust came up to their shoulders. It was also very windy there. We would try to put down nets and tarps, but the wind blew them all away. We could not keep the babies' noses and eyes clean. Red dust would come out everywhere. It covered our dry skin.

When we cooked, we put water in our pots, and covered them, and then the winds would come and blow the covers off and fill the water full of dust. We would dump the water and put in more, and the same thing would happen until we got sick of it and just put the flour into the water with the dust. The white flour became red with the dust. We just ate our dusty red food.

We all found a tree to live under and prayed for relief from this dust that filled our world. We also had no good water. One month later it rained. It hadn't rained for years. We finally had gotten our miracle.

With the dust settled down, this became a good camp. We built our huts there. We received food and water from the UN, and we settled in and tried to heal. For a time all was well. My young siblings Bok, Nyanluok, and Mareach were with us in this camp, and being together gave us strength. I remember some of the children playing wedding behind my hut. Atong was a singer while the little ones acted out the wedding.

This was the time of the beans. The Red Cross gave us beans that were so tough we had to cook them all day. By evening, they would still be too hard for the little children to eat, because their teeth had not yet come in. We would have to pound them with a mortar and pestle and then grind them between two stones before the children could eat them. That became my fulltime job. When Kut was too hungry to wait, I would chew the beans for him. Kut would drink Jok's milk. When we took him to the nutrition center, Kut would get nothing because, as he said, "They think I'm fat." A child got a bracelet at the feeding center if he or she didn't weigh enough.

Jok was still very sick. I needed to take him to a better hospital. I decided to go to Nairobe City to look for my brother-in-law, Bior.

While we were still in Narus, Bior had invited my daughter and my cousin to join him in Nairobe, where he was working with the SPLA. He sent a message that he wanted to take care of my cousin Abeny, because her husband, a cousin of his, had died. My husband was also related to Bior, but not so closely. Bior wanted to help me by taking my daughter Atong to live with him and his wife. Atong was only five years old. Bior thought that Abeny could care for Atong and Atong could go to school. I would have an easier time providing for the others in the camp at Narus, where there was no school. This may sound strange to some readers, but our people would have considered it an appropriate arrangement. Bior's wife was not happy with the idea, however, so I did not want to do it.

One of Bior's sisters was with us in Narus. She jumped up when she heard of his invitation and said, "No. None of you is going there. When you start your farm, you don't start it far away. You start it near your hut. This is how you start to clear your farm. So I don't want you to go to my brother." What she meant was that she was related to Bior much more closely than Abeny and Atong, so Bior should be helping her and her children instead of us.

I told her I was not going to her brother's and neither was my daughter. I knew a story about the snake: When people burn the jungle, the snakes die in the fire. A family of snakes will group themselves to die together. The mother puts herself on her babies and they all burn together. I told that example to my sister-in-law. I told her, "I am not going to let my daughter go to your brother. I want to die with my children like a snake. I am going to die with my children." It was bad enough that my husband died and part of my body was buried while the other part of my body was alive. I didn't want any other part of my body to be buried somewhere else. That's what I told my relatives.

So I lived in Kakuma for two years until Jok became so sick that I knew I must leave to find treatment for him. I went to the camp manager and told him my son and other children in my family were very sick. I asked if he could help me go to Nairobi to live with a relative and find treatment for my son. The camp manager told me he would think about it. I kept going to his office every day. The children had high fevers every night, so he agreed to come to see the children himself. When he came, he could see that they were all skin and bones and he said he would let me go. My youngest brother, Mareach, was very sick, but the camp manager told me I could not take him with me. I took him anyway.

The manager told me to go to another man who was working in the compound. I talked to that other man, and the next day he came with a car. He told me that I was leaving then because the camp manager had approved my papers. So I grabbed Mareach and my three children. The man took us to the UN compound a few miles away from the refugee camp and told me to wait under a certain tree.

A Kenyan woman who worked with the UN came to us there under the tree. She told me to wait there for a truck. She gave me five hundred Kenyan shillings. She said, "This is for you." Some other people came and asked me what she gave me, and I told them five hundred Kenyan shillings. I had never seen five hundred, and I thought it was a lot of money. These two people came and asked me what she gave me, and I told them money. They wanted to know how much, and I told them five hundred. They said no, that it was not five hundred because that was not what she was supposed to give me. She was supposed to give me four thousand shillings. I said, "Well, this is good enough." These people complained that she didn't give me the right amount of money. But I didn't complain. I didn't care. I just wanted to go somewhere to get treatment for my baby.

After awhile, a big truck came, a long truck with a plastic cover over the back. The back was empty, so the children and I got in. We walked all the way to the front, close to the driver, and sat down. We couldn't see into the front of the truck. Three people were riding there: two Kenyan men and a white woman.

The truck went first into the town of Kakuma and stopped. The white woman came to us in the back of the truck and asked if we were hungry. We were very hungry. She went to the market and bought us things. It was the first time we tasted Pepsi. She brought us four bottles of Pepsi, some bread, and lots of other food. The children were so happy. We were all smiling at that white woman. We already had a life change. We ate and the children tasted this and tasted that and then the truck left.

At our next stop, the driver told us to come down from the truck. So we all got out of the truck and he filled it with sacks and sacks of black coal. There was almost no room for us in there. We got in, and I said to myself, "Oh my, how am I going to fit in here with all this coal?" When the truck started moving again, the road was bumpy, throwing us up and down. Sacks of coal started to hit us. We were turning black with coal dust. The dust was in the children's eyes. Whenever the truck hit a bump, heavy sacks would land on the children. I would stand up and push the sacks back, and then I would fall down. We traveled like that all night.

The children were trying to sleep but couldn't. We all had eye problems now because of all the dust from the coal. Our bodies were very, very black. Finally the truck stopped and the white woman came to see how we were doing. When she saw that the truck was full of coal, she became very angry with the men. She asked me what had happened, and I said the men had put all this coal into the truck, and now we were black and sick. She looked at the baby's eyes, and the baby could not see. She yelled at the men and told them to remove the sacks. They were not supposed to have that coal. They had smuggled it into the truck to sell in Nairobi for their own profit. The white woman made them clear out the truck right away. I was so happy with her. She said we were not going any farther that day, because the children needed rest. She told them to find a hotel for us. Oh, thank God for the white woman. I will never forget her.

They found us a room with a single bed. I took the blanket from the bed and put it on the floor for the children. The four of us could not all fit in that single bed. The truck driver and his friend didn't know the white lady was coming back. I lay on the floor with my daughter, and I let my brother and my son sleep on the bed. Before we went to sleep, the white woman came back. When she saw our room, she said, "Oh my God! They did it again! They put you in one bed!" She went and yelled at them again. Then she found us a room with two big double beds. She yelled at the driver again, and then she came with medicine for our eyes before we went to bed. She said goodnight to us, and she was so sweet. She was my angel. I said, "God, how did you send this angel to us? I knew you had angels." God sent that angel to me and my children to protect us on our way to Nairobi. In the morning when she came, our eyes felt better. The baby could see. The white woman smiled at the baby, and she held him, and the baby smiled. I knew she was an angel. When I see white women now I feel like one of them is the angel that God sent to me. I know I have a white angel.

Nairobi

We arrived in Nairobi the next day. The white woman asked if I knew where I was going, and I said that I didn't, but that any black Sudanese would be able to tell me where to go. The white woman asked some people where the Sudanese were, and they directed her to a building where Sudanese people lived. She took us there, and I told her that we would be just fine there. So I thanked my angel and told her that God would bless her. Then she left with the truck, and I have neither seen nor heard of her since.

We were treated very well in that house because I knew the woman of that house from before. Saida was the wife of a leader of the southern Sudanese people, a man named William. It was the first time for me to go to a big city like that, and I was in a big house with many lady's maids. Some were ironing and washing children's clothes, and some were cooking for Saida. My children and I were looking all around the rooms. It was a big, beautiful house. Saida came down and said hello to me and told me there were people who would serve us. Then she went back upstairs to her room. She was an important lady. Servants gave us food and drink, and asked if my children needed a bath. I said they did, so they took my children and bathed them. We waited in the living room until Saida came back down some two hours later. She told me I could stay there with her, but I said that I had come to see my husband's cousin and that my baby was sick and needed treatment. She said that if I stayed in the house with her maybe she could help me, but I said no, that I needed to go to my relative.

Saida's husband William led a splinter group of Sudanese who had fallen out with the SPLA. Relations between the two groups were very hostile. Therefore, no one from Saida's house could go to my brother-in-law's house. Saida knew of a *maiz,* a house rented by a group of people, that was home to SPLA officers. She sent a servant to find us a taxi, and she paid the taxi driver and sent us on our way. No one from her home dared go to the SPLA home.

The *maiz* was empty except for one man, but I happened to know him by reputation because he was from Bor. He knew a relative of my brother-in-law's wife who could take me to their house.

When I knocked on my brother-in-law's gate, one of the children came running and opened it for us. We went in and sat down, and Bior's wife came. We knew each other, and we hugged. Because I was wearing the white dress for grieving, she cried and then told me to sit there and she would come back. She brought us water and showed me the room where I was supposed to stay. In the evening the food was made and we ate. And we stayed there.

In the morning, Bior sent a little boy to tell me that he needed me in the living room. I expected him to say he was sorry for me because my husband was killed. I expected him to ask how I was doing and how the kids were doing and what we had experienced running from place to place as refugees. But I did not get what I expected. Instead he asked me why I had come there. I looked at him like, "What question is this?" So he asked me again about why I came. So I told him that one of the children was very sick, and I had just lost one, and I didn't want this other child to die, so I had come to look for treatment. He asked me, "Don't you know Nairobi is a big city and you cannot just come here? Where can you get treatment?" He started yelling at me. Then he told me I could go back to my room.

I got up very disappointed, humiliated, and sad. I got up, and I left. I went to my room and started crying. I said, "So when your husband dies, you will be rejected, huh? By the relatives, by the world, by everybody. You will be rejected by everybody." I went to my room and cried. I started getting fever right away because of the situation. I started getting sick from the day that I heard that yelling from my relative.

The next morning I didn't know what to do until Bior's wife came and told me that we needed to go to the UN office. I needed to get documents there attesting that I was a refugee in Nairobi. We went there and I got the documents and I got a Visa for three months. She told me that this was my document, and I could stay for three months, but when it expired, I had to take it back there so I could get it renewed.

I had left the refugee camp with nothing but what I was wearing— just that one white dress. No change of underwear, no shoes, no nothing. The same was true for the kids. Each of us had just one set of ragged clothes. So we just stayed like that. Months later, when my menstrual period started, I went to Bior's wife and asked her if she could help me with underwear, and she gave me some of hers, and I thanked her. I tried it on, but it was loose because I was just skin and bones. So I tied it on one side, really tight, and I just wore it like that.

In the refugee camps, we made toothbrushes from pieces of a certain kind of tree. You go and grab three or four pieces of that tree. It smells so good. You chew on the side of it and make it soft and then you can brush your teeth with it. But I forgot to bring my brush from the refugee camp at Kakuma. So when I got to Nairobi my teeth were hurting. Every day I got up and didn't brush, and my teeth hurt. So one day I went to a woman who lived in the house and was also related to my husband, and I asked her to share her toothbrush with me. She said OK. So every morning I would wait for her to brush first, and then after she brushed, I washed the toothbrush and then brushed my teeth with it. Sometimes she clearly didn't like it, but she had to give it to me because I needed it. I had to ask her. She didn't have to share it, but I had to beg her for it so I could brush my teeth. So we shared her toothbrush for a few months.

I had a home, but I had nothing. At meals, a maid would bring us food, but it was very small portions for the children and me. She would bring some to Jok and Kut first and then some small scraps to Mareach and Atong. She served me last, and when I went to eat, Mareach and Atong would watch me, and I would give some of my food to them. Some days I gave it all away and ate nothing. That is how we lived.

I was very sick with malaria from the day my relative yelled at me. One of the women in the house noticed how sick I was, so one night she brought me very strong medicine. I don't know where she found it, but she told me to take four of the pills. I swallowed them, but because I was so very sick, that medicine almost killed me. I almost died that night. I passed out on the bed but woke up on the floor, and my sister-in-law that I shared the toothbrush with took me to the hospital.

I had papers from the Red Cross that said I was eligible for treatment. The doctor told me, "You look very sick." He wanted to do some tests, especially for HIV. I knew I didn't have HIV, and I told him I had malaria. He said, "No, you look like you have HIV." They took my blood and he told me to come back in three days.

When I went back, I was vomiting along the way, and it was horrible. The doctor told me I was right: I didn't have HIV, but I had chronic malaria and needed treatment. So I asked him about my son, who was also very sick. The doctor told me to bring all the children.

They found that my daughter had tuberculosis, and the other children all had malaria. The doctor said that we would have to stay in Nairobi for eight months of treatment. I told him I couldn't stay that long in Nairobi, but he insisted that the baby needed treatment for eight months.

So I stayed, but in Bior's house the situation was really bad. They did not have enough food, and he was not happy with me. He told me to go back to the refugee camp. I told him my son needed treatment for eight months. He told me I could not stay, but I asked him to let me stay until I was done with my malaria medicine. I was getting a shot every morning. He refused, but I stayed anyway.

After a while, I found some neighbors who were relatives. I would walk to their house to drink tea to satisfy a little of my hunger. I had no shoes, so I would wait for the women in the house to leave so I could use their sandals. They would put on nice shoes and leave the sandals by the door, and I would grab a pair of sandals and run to the neighbor so I could have tea. Then I would come back quickly so when the women came back, the sandals would be there.

One day out of the blue the wife of the former SPLA President, Doctor John Garang De Mabior, came to visit Bior's house. We all knew her as Mama Rebecca. I had never met her but had heard all about her when we were in Ethiopia. As she visited with people in the house, she learned that the wife of the late Akech Jok had come there from Kakuma. She asked to be shown to my room, and she stood in my door and greeted me. I recognized her but was surprised. What was the wife of the big leader doing at my door? She sat by me and asked about my situation. She spoke to me really nicely and promised to help me get Atong into school in Nairobi and keep her there. She said she'd talk to Bior about my situation. Then she opened her purse and took out five thousand Kenyan shillings and gave them to me. It was only the second time I had seen Kenyan shillings. It was a lot of money. She told me she was related to my husband, and she invited me to visit her in her home.

Later I visited Mama Rebecca with my sister-in-law Aluel. She greeted us in a friendly way and hosted us generously. She urged me to stay at Bior's house, but I told her I would need to move on to find a way to support my children. She listened and advised me as I talked to her about my future. She was worried about the dangers for us in refugee camps but seemed to understand that the camps were a route for us out of our dire situation. I am still grateful for her help and attention as I gathered my strength for my next move.

One day Bior came to me and told me to go back to the refugee camp. I told him that I didn't want to go to the refugee camp, I wanted to go somewhere else. I wanted to go to a different refugee camp. He argued and yelled at me again. I had nowhere to go. It was like living in a cage in that house.

Luckily some people were there who had come from a different refugee camp, and they had been my husband's students. I told them that my husband had been killed, and they said they were sorry. They told me that my husband was a funny teacher and a good teacher. Then they asked me why I was there looking so bad, so very skinny. I told them about coming to Nairobi for treatment and about how Bior had treated me and that I had nowhere to go. One of the students told me that the refugee camp that they had just left was taking widows for resettlement to Canada. If I went there, maybe I could get into that program.

One of them said not to tell me that, because Somali rebels were preying on travelers along the way to that camp. I could be killed. They started to argue. One said that maybe God would be with me and nothing would happen. He said to look at me: I was not going to make it in Nairobi. And if I died, who would take care of my children? So again they started to argue. I listened to the one who said, "Let her go. Maybe God will help her."

Those people came every day to Bior's house. They told me Canada was sponsoring people to emigrate there. I was very excited. They said that in Canada life is really good. You wouldn't have to work; they would just support you and give you assistance. In the United States, you would work really hard, and life would be hard. I was happy to go to Canada. In a couple of days, Bior left for Egypt for his work. I left his house and Nairobi soon afterward. If he had been there, he might have forced me to go back to the refugee camp at Kakuma.

My sister-in-law Aluel left with me on the bus. We spent the night on the border from Somalia and Kenya. The next day we tried to walk, but it was very difficult because we were in a deep jungle. We sat down on the grass and put down our mosquito net, and we stayed the night there. We didn't know what would protect us, but I knew it was God. Otherwise in the deep jungle, no one will protect you.

Applications for resettlement were given out only infrequently. We had heard that it was nearly application time, so if we waited, we might miss out on the process of resettlement. At the border with Somalia, refugees usually waited for an army convoy to ensure their safe travel. We had no time to wait. The morning after we arrived at the border, we took a truck. We took a big risk taking one of the small trucks, because they were often attacked by rebels. We might have waited for a bus to come along with a big army truck to lead it down the road, but we took the first truck that came along: a small one. That is what got us into trouble.

We huddled together in the back of the truck. Most of the people were Somalis and Ethiopians. Aluel sat near me. I held the baby, Jok, and Kut, Atong, and Mareach were plastered to my side. A bunch of men sat above us on the metal framework that held a plastic tarpaulin in bad weather. Suddenly I heard a shot, the truck stopped, and men rained down upon us. "Get off my children!" I shouted at them, and I shoved them away. "Aluel, come help me get these men off the children!" I was so preoccupied with that problem that I did not see the bigger one. Then I noticed two Somali rebels climbing onto our truck. We had been captured. Our driver was already lying on the ground with rifles to his head.

The two Somalis on the truck waved their guns to tell us to get off. We found ourselves surrounded by men and boys with guns. They wore long white robes and their heads were wrapped in dingy white scarves, revealing only their eyes. They all carried long black guns, which they held to our heads. They took all our clothes except our underwear.

We stood waiting for the shots that would mix all our blood. Guns to our heads, our eyes closed, we prayed for our end, which was directly upon us. We opened our eyes to the miracle of life. No one was killed, and we were allowed to proceed.

Our next stop was a small town where police and UN workers interviewed us. They wanted to know about the rebel bandits. Then we were taken to the UN compound and given tents, cooking utensils, and food. Then we were taken to the camp.

IFO Refugee Camp

We straggled into the IFO refugee camp in our underwear, hearts scarred by fear, but still alive. IFO is a UN camp on the Somalia-Kenya border. It turned out to be our last stop before America.

Many Somali refugees were in this camp, making it dangerous, because Somali rebels would come at night to rob them. In many cases, these bandits killed their victims. This camp was in the desert, so we could not find the materials we needed to make our huts. The UN provided tents and some food.

Here we got food every fifteen days. The food lasted for eight. Throughout the week before the next food distribution, we ate leaves. Our lack of clothes was a hardship, but malnutrition was worse. My daughter was six years old, and she suffered the most from the lack of nutrition. For some reason my two boys were fine until my two-year-old got malaria. He was admitted to the hospital, but with medicine he got better. I also had malaria.

The beans were full of bugs. One time we got some beans that had a different kind of bugs, not the kind we were used to. Our usual bugs would float to the top of the water, and we could scoop them out. This time, one of the young guys from a near-by camp came to me and said, "Have you seen the new kind of bugs? Not the black bugs we eat every day, but white ones." That made me laugh.

We spent a year in IFO. We were waiting either to go or to die. Things were not good there, but I was able to enjoy the kids. Jok talked when he was very young. He would tell me when he needed to breast-feed. Once when he was about two years old, two men came to visit and I was standing, making tea. Jok was trying to breast-feed while he was standing. The men said, "Why is this boy still breast-feeding? Is it because of the war?" Jok took his mouth off and said, "Don't you see, there is no food here. It is not because of the war." The men thought that was terribly funny.

Jok would say, "I am not going to stop breast-feeding until I go to America." He called white people *UN*. He did not like them because they gave him shots. He said, "No shots, give us food."

We had a rope strung between two trees for a clothesline. Jok would swing on it. One day he was swinging and yelling, "My God, help me!" I had no idea why he was saying that. Everyone around us was laughing. After that, everyone knew that Jok had found God. A young man named Johnny asked Jok to ask his god to help Johnny when he interviewed for permission to go to the United States. Jok said no. He thought that Johnny's god could help Johnny. Jok would not ask Jok's god to do it.

Kut was very funny. He would tell everyone he was an American man. We all knew about America even through we didn't know where it was. All the men in the camp called him the *American Man*. Kut was not afraid of anything. Even when he was a year old he would grab onto a goat as it came out of a pen and hold on. He was very brave. After he learned to crawl, he would dump our food and play in it. Then we would have no food that day. One day at Iteng he dumped the gas from the lantern into the jug of milk. He had a bad habit of hitting other children with a spoon. The girls had to hide the spoons from him.

Mareach was the youngest boy. When we went to get our food rations, we had to wait in line a long time. People would wait three days for rations of sugar, flour, oil, and salt. Mareach learned to speak Swahili, so that he could smooth talk the guards. "My mother just had a baby, so we really need our food," he would say, and the guards would let him in. Then the guards would tell him to get someone to help him carry the heavy rations. Mareach would bring the Dinka men who were our friends and tell the guards that they were his uncles and that they must have their rations too so that they would be free to help him carry our food. The Kenyans also loved him. He would chat up the guards even when it was not ration time. He told them that his sister was his mom, and they were intrigued by his story. Everybody loved him in the camp.

Once when Kut was sick, I took him to the hospital. It was full of children who were sick and dying there all day and night. Jok was still breast-feeding, so I had him with me. A Dinka man from Paleek offered to stay with Kut through the night so that Jok would not have to be there with all the sick children. I would come every morning so that the man could go back to the camp for breakfast.

Children were dying in our camp. One morning a little girl from the Acholi tribe died. Her name was Lucy. She used to come to our tent to play with our children. She was a beautiful little girl of six or seven years. Her mom would send her to ask me for firewood or salt or oil. She called me Auntie. She was sick for only two days. One day she didn't come to our tent, so I asked her older sister Jessica about her and learned she was sick. Two days later she was dead. We were all shocked. A few days later an infant died. Kut was still in the hospital with chronic malaria. We already had four graves of children inside our gate.

I was waiting for my name to come up on the list of people who were to be interviewed for passage to America. I had gotten onto a list of people who were to meet with a JVA official for the first of two interviews that would clear me for immigration to the United States. Before my name came up on the list, one of the Dinka guys from a neighboring tent came to me. He was one of the men who had been volunteering to dig the graves for the children. He told me that a Dinka woman's name had come up on the list. She had left the camp a long time ago, so he urged me to go in her place for her interview. He sounded very emotional. I was stirring a pot and had my back to him as he spoke. Shocked at his idea, I whirled and asked him why I should do that. "We don't want to bury Kut here," he said. "Just answer when they call her name." One by one, Dinka men from our gate came into my tent and urged me to do that.

I didn't like doing it, because I value truth so much, but I went to the JVA office and when they called her name, I answered it. I became Rebecca Nomngeek. All those Dinka men were standing outside peering through the window and praying for me and my children. The lady who was giving out information sheets asked, "Are you Rebecca?" and I said yes. She sent us to have our photos taken, and when we came out she gave me a document with all our names on it, and I was formally accepted for the crucial interview. The Dinka men outside the window cheered. I was unhappy about my deceit, but when I looked at the graves inside our gate, I knew that I had had no choice.

Later, when I was in Nairobi, I looked for the real Rebecca Nomngeek. "Are you crazy?" said my friends. Some of them were in tears over the risk I was taking. I wanted to be honest with her, though, so I went to her and told her what I had done.

I offered to go back to JVA and confess what I had done, but she said that she had married and was living a good life. "Just take your children and be me," she said. I thanked her with all my heart. We have become very good friends.

After I had arrived in the United States, I went to court and changed my name to Abeny Kucha—my real name. Back in IFO, when my name finally came up on the interview list, another woman took it. She went to Canada. I knew her. I talked to her on the phone after she immigrated, and I asked whether she had changed her name. "Why would I do that?" she replied. So her name is also Abeny Kucha.

After I had passed the first interview, we waited for three or four months for the next one. It was conducted by lawyers. The refugees would watch the JVA offices for the lawyers' cars, and when they appeared, word would spread through the camp. We knew that interviews started the next day. When I went for my interview, I took all the children and waited until my name was called. I walked into the interview room and saw a bald white man sitting at a table on the other side of the room. I had heard that he was the toughest of several lawyers who were conducting interviews that time. I was so nervous I was sweating. He spoke very sternly and never smiled. He told me to stand against the wall facing him all the way across the room. "Why do you want to go to America?" he asked. "Who is Mareach? Where was your husband killed?" That was all there was to my interview.

Later I asked the interpreter, "Now what?"

"Now," said the interpreter, "you wait for the letter." The *calling letter* informs you that you have passed the interview and must take a medical exam before you can be admitted to the United States. It goes on with all these good words and then ends with "Good luck!" All the letters arrive at the JVA office at the same time, so those of us who had interviewed at the same time all went to the office to pick up our letters. The Dinka men who had attended my first interview gathered outside the office and watched to see how I would react to my letter. They thought I might kill myself if we were rejected, so they were there to support me. People who were rejected took it very hard. It was said that two men had committed suicide upon receiving letters of rejection.

I could not stand to wait for the JVA to take my group to Nairobi for the medical exam. I sold my ration card and paid our own way. At first I stayed with one of my sisters in Nairobi, but the situation was very bad in her house, so I decided to visit the camp where my group was going to stay. It had a Swahili name that was something like Ruyuru. I found a woman at the camp who would share her tent with us, so I went back for the kids and moved to the camp. Our hostess shared her food with us.

Sanitation was terrible in that camp. Our blankets and mattresses had been used before and were full of lice. When my group arrived from IFO, we were permitted to eat food prepared by the staff. It was not well cooked and gave us diarrhea. I learned to cook it again after we received it. People fought for tents. I had to move my family to a JVA building that was used for reception of new refugees.

We were in the camp from late March till May. The medical exam was easy. We took a bus from the camp to the hospital. We came back in the evening. Then we waited two weeks for the results of our chest x-rays and tests on blood, urine, and stool. The JVA posted a list of people who were to go to the hospital to receive their results. Nobody said a word as we rode to this final reckoning. The doctor gave me medicine for parasites but told me that we were fine. Another lady and her husband came back sad, and we all knew not to ask. A week later our names were posted on a list of people who were going to the United States.

Going to America

We were so happy the day we left the refugee camp, because we had been waiting such a long time with no food or medical care. God chose for me and my children to leave on May 24, 1994. That day we were waiting for the bus to come and pick us up. While we waited, we all stayed very busy. I was cooking, and some of the other refugees too, because we were worried that the kids would be hungry on the way. We didn't even know that there would be food in the plane. It was raining, and we didn't have a stove. We just cooked over an open fire. We had a very hard time keeping the fire going with wet wood. We were in a tent. The kids were crying. It was a very difficult day, but we were happy.

Around 3:00 the bus came, and we were waiting in the line. The kids were very excited to be getting into the bus. The JVA people told us to wait and they would call our names one by one. I was thirtieth on the list. My little boy, two years old, was crying really hard because he wanted to get on the bus. He was sick of the situation there. A man said to me, "Why don't you let this baby go in the bus?"

I said, "These people will not let me." So he took my baby's hand and said, "Go in." So my little boy jumped in the bus. They helped him. He was just by himself and all the people were waiting for their names to be called. My little boy was the first one in the bus and he was only two years old. He went in there and he climbed onto a seat and just sat there. I watched him through the window and waved to him. So the people in charge decided to let me board the bus because that baby could not just sit there by himself. So they let me in with my other children while everybody else got on. As the bus pulled away, my heart was beating really bad, and I wasn't sure why. Was it because I was leaving home, or because I was going to a better place?

At the Nairobi airport people helped us through the process of boarding the flight. I had never taken a commercial flight before. I was carrying only the plastic bag that had all of our documents. It was me and four children—my three children and my brother who was eleven years old. He was the oldest. My daughter was eight. My little boys were three and a half and two and a half. So it was just us and a plastic bag I was carrying.

After all the process was done, we went into the plane. I thought it was just a small room at the end of a narrow hallway. Mareach felt the vibration from the engines and said, "I think this is the plane."

As the plane left the airport, I looked down and saw all the lights and the houses and the buildings. I looked down and I felt sorry for myself because my heart told me, "This is home, and now you are leaving, and you don't even know where you are going." So I prayed. With tears in my eyes, I said, "God, take me wherever you want me to go. Wherever you choose for me." Then after I prayed, my heartbeat was calm, and my children fell asleep. I started to sing a Dinka song, "Lord, Let Us Leave with Blessing," that I learned in church when I was young. My uncle explained that song to me, that it was sung by people who were taken as slaves. So that song is a Christian song for the people who left the country a long time ago. They were asking God to protect them on the way. So I sang that song in my heart while I was on the plane with the children:

Lord, let us leave with blessing;
Accept our humble hearts and peace.
Feel us with Your love and take away our tiredness
When we are walking on this path.
We thank You and we worship You with the good words we heard
from You.
Let us call on You with a good prayer in our hearts and in our lives.

I could hardly wrap my mind around the changes that were about to happen in my life. All my troubles seem to happen in May, that dark month of new beginnings. I was very nervous about leaving my homeland where I was born with laughter. Now the laughter was replaced with the hollow ache of hunger and the dark vision of death and constant fear. I was tired down to my very soul. America seemed so bright it hurt my eyes. May was the shadow that fell across the sun. I gathered courage around my battered mind and looked toward my one chance at life.

Chapter 6: America

It was a long, long traveling until we reached New York. I never knew which airport we landed at. We refugees had no experience in cities, so we had a hard time on the escalator. People were falling down. Security saw our problem and announced that the escalator should be stopped, so they stopped the escalator for us. People from the International Organization for Migration (IOM) had to show us how to use the toilets in the restrooms.

We arrived early in the morning. Some IOM people took us to a lounge area. It was the children and me and lots of other refugees. We stayed in that lounge until our flight out that afternoon. At lunchtime the IOM people showed us to an airport restaurant. My sandwich tasted like soap. I threw it away. I tried pizza and it was nasty. The kids ate everything with no problems. They learned their way around the airport and soon were showing the adults where to go and what to do.

One lady and I had some women's problems there, and we kept talking to each other like, "What are we going to do?" We didn't even have a change of clothes. We had a very hard time at that place because we needed some women's supplies like pads, and we didn't know the names so we could not ask for help. So we used paper towels and stood up the whole time we were there.

The time change had made us very tired. When it was afternoon in New York, it was the middle of the night in Nairobi. We all needed sleep. Some people wanted to go back to Africa. We were tired of all this waiting and discomfort.

Around three o'clock that afternoon, a man came and called my name and told us to follow him. I said goodbye to the friends I had made there and have never seen them again. The man led us to our flight and went with us onto the plane. When we were settled and belted into our seats, he waved goodbye to us and left. Before he left, I asked him where we were going. "Portland, Maine," he said. Before we left Africa, I had gone through an orientation, but I did not pay attention to where I was going. Maybe they told me, but I did not remember it. So I did not know about Portland, Maine, until we boarded the plane.

Portland, Maine

We landed in Portland around five o'clock in the afternoon. We got out of the plane with other people. The person who was supposed to receive us was late, so everyone from our flight left the airport, and I found myself just standing there with my children not knowing where I was going. I felt like a lost ship.

I saw some chairs and a couch, and I told my children, "Let's go and sit. Maybe someone will come and find us." While I was sitting there my baby started crying, so I just gave him my breast.

The baby started feeding, and a woman came running and said, "No, you cannot do that here! You need to go somewhere."

I didn't know what she was talking about. My breast was just outside there. That's how we do it where I came from. I asked her what she was saying.

She said, "You need to cover and hide in the bathroom."

I said, "Who am I hiding? Is it the baby or the breast?" It was something I didn't know.

Two social workers finally arrived to take us to our new home. They led us to the baggage claim. Everyone else from our flight was taking bags from the moving belt. One of the social workers asked me, "Did you see your luggage here?"

And I said, "Oh, I don't have any luggage."

She said, "Oh, my gosh. You don't have anything?"

I said, "Just this plastic bag with the papers in it." So we went to the car.

They put us into two cars. Mareach and Atong rode with one of the women, and Jok and Kut and I with the other. The car I was in had two car seats for the little boys, but I didn't know what they were. So she told me that the boys would sit in these car seats. I said OK, and we put the boys in the car seats, and Jok was crying. When the social worker asked me why he was still crying, I said it was because he was hungry because I didn't have a chance to breast-feed him.

She said, "He is still breast-feeding at nearly three years old?"

We drove to a place called the Welcome House. Quickly, she showed me around. She opened the refrigerator and said, "This is your food." She showed me the bathroom and the rooms for the children, and she told me that we would stay there until they found me an apartment. She told me about the telephone. There were some numbers beside it with the office number, her number, and 911 for emergencies. And she told me, "This is the smoke detector. It is a fire alarm. When you hear it, you run outside. Don't try to take anything. Just go outside." She showed me everything very quickly, and then she left.

There we were, standing in the middle of the living room not knowing what to do. We had just arrived from Africa. We didn't have a room, a hut, nothing. We were wondering what to do now. So I told them to sit down. Everyone sat down for a little while, and then everyone stood up. We were confused and exhausted and we didn't know where we were. I told the kids, "Let's sit down."

I went to the kitchen and found some pop in big bottles. In Africa, the big bottles are for juice and the small ones are for Pepsi, so we thought it was juice. Actually it was Coca Cola and orange pop. I poured the orange into glasses and gave it to the kids. It was something we had never tasted before, and we didn't like it, so we left it there.

I went back to the refrigerator. I recognized milk, but I tasted it first before I gave it to the kids. The milk was very cold, so I warmed it up. The lady had shown me how to turn on the stove, but I had never used a stove before so it took me a long time to turn it on. I had seen an electric stove in Nairobi, but I had been told that gas stoves were dangerous and often set people on fire. I was scared and shaking as I worked to turn on that stove. I thought that firewood would be easier than this. When the fire finally popped up, I jumped back and ran. When I finally had the milk warm, I had a tough time turning the stove off again. The small things, when I was new, were very difficult for me.

Before we could drink our warm milk, a lady came to the door. The social worker who had shown me around the house had not told me about the doorbell. She *had* told me about the smoke detector and fire alarm. So when this lady rang the door bell, I told the kids that this was the fire alarm that the lady had told us about, and we needed to run outside. So we did.

We had a plan when we were in refugee camps. If we heard the sound of guns or anything coming, my daughter would hold my skirt, my younger brother would take the baby, I would take the three-year-old, and we would run. This was still the plan. I told the kids on the plane that when we got to America, we would keep our plan. We didn't know where we were going, and maybe it would be a bad place too. So when the door bell rang, I grabbed the three-year-old, my brother grabbed the baby, my daughter grabbed my dress, and we all ran outside. We were upstairs, so we ran downstairs and out the door. We pushed the door so hard we almost knocked the lady down who was ringing the doorbell.

She jumped out of our way and gave us a puzzled look. We ran past her and across the street, and there we stood, looking toward the top of the building, expecting to see fire, but there was no fire. I asked the kids if they saw fire on the building but they didn't. I asked them if smelled smoke, but they didn't. We stood there for more than an hour. We were lucky that it was May and not very cold.

Eventually, I told the kids that we should go back inside, because we didn't know where else to go, and we didn't see any fire. We went back into the building. We remembered that we had come from upstairs, but we had been there only some thirty minutes before we evacuated, and we couldn't remember which apartment was ours. We didn't ever know the apartments had numbers on their doors. Most of the doors were closed, but we saw one that was open, so we thought this might be the one we had come out of. Slowly, I crept in and looked around. I told the kids to wait by the door. Nobody was in the apartment. Because we didn't have anything, we had nothing to recognize our apartment by. After awhile, my brother remembered that he had opened a bar of soap in the bathroom. He was able to find a bar of soap that he recognized, so that was how we found our apartment. We smelled the soap to make sure it was the same bar he had opened. We were very lucky that there was soap in the bathroom so we could recognize our apartment.

We were very nervous, and I told my family that we were not going to sleep in different rooms because we had never slept in different rooms. We had always slept together in a single hut in case something happened at night. That way we could all run together. We took the mattresses from the beds and put them on the floor, and all five of us slept in the same room. We were very comfortable, but the rest of the house was empty.

In the morning Ellen McKenzie, the social worker, came to take us to the government center so we could get our documents. We did a lot of paperwork there. When she took us home, she told me that we had an appointment the next day at the hospital to have our check-ups. She said the taxi would come so we would need to be ready for it. I got up at five o'clock and got the kids ready. The taxi came and took us to the hospital, but nobody was there to show us where to go. I saw people going into the elevator, and I had never been in an elevator before in my life. I took the kids onto the elevator when I saw people going in. The elevator went up. Everyone was pushing the number where they were going, but I didn't know the number where I was going, so we went all the way up to the top floor and then came down. People kept getting out and I just stood there with the kids. We went up and down at least four times until a man noticed that we never got off. He asked me where we were going, so I showed him the papers I was carrying. He told me I needed to get out on the third floor, and he offered to take me there. Luckily I had found help.

When the elevator opened, I was nervous, and I couldn't get out. In my heart I was thinking, "How did I get myself into this with the children?" And the children were just looking at me. I could not say one word because I was so nervous. The man took me to the correct room and up to the desk and showed my papers. A nurse received us, and we were very happy. Still, I was shivering and nervous and my heart was beating fast. But no one knew: just me and my God.

When our check-ups were finished, the nurse took us to the place where we could wait for the taxi. Luckily I had gotten the help we needed. God just told these people, "This woman doesn't know what she is doing! She doesn't know where she is or what is going on in the whole world!"

We spent four months in Portland—a very difficult four months. I didn't know anybody until I met a Sudanese man at the Catholic Charities office. We were both there for an orientation. He attended an Episcopal church, and I was an Episcopal, so he invited me to go to his church. At church I found another nice man, a lawyer named Charlie March. One night he visited us in our apartment. I was very sick with a kidney infection, so he took me to the hospital. He and his wife Robyn stayed with me in the hospital all night. He was a lawyer, and he was helping. He came back to the apartment the next morning after I had gotten home from the hospital, and he cooked for the children. I didn't believe a lawyer would do that. He was a lawyer and he was a Christian—a very good believer. After that he always came to take me to church. The first way I knew since I came to America was a church. And he came and took me to church all the time.

After four months, I met a Sudanese woman at the orientation office. She had come to the United States before me so she knew the telephone numbers of other Sudanese in the States. She spoke to some Sudanese who were from my tribe. They were in Rochester, Minnesota. I was homesick and missed speaking with people in my own language. I also missed the food. The social worker could take me shopping for groceries, but I couldn't find what I needed because I didn't know the English names of things. Especially okra. I was so hungry for okra. I didn't know the name of it. I was so hungry for my home food. So this Sudanese lady told some Sudanese in Rochester, "You guys have a lady here who is Sudanese, and she is a single mother with children, and she is really suffering here. She doesn't know anybody, and she is suffering with the kids."

Once when she came to visit me she saw me washing the children's clothes in the bathtub because I didn't know about the washer and dryer. I had been drying clothes on the couch every night. So this lady felt sorry for me and told the Sudanese Dinkas in Rochester, "You guys need to help her move there so she can be with you, so you can show her everything she needs." She gave them my telephone number.

One of the men called me. He told me, "We heard about you there, and we know you are having a hard time with the children."

I just cried when I heard his voice on the phone, because I knew him. We had been in the IFO refugee camp together. I cried into the phone and said, "Why do you guys let me suffer like this? I am lost. I feel like I am lost."

He said, "Don't cry. We will find a way to bring you here. You will move here to stay with us. There are three families here, and you can be together with us." I was so happy that night, because I had spoken with someone who spoke my dialect and someone I had known before.

It wasn't that I didn't have a good time in Portland; I did have a good time there, but sometimes when you are among people you don't know and people who don't speak your language, you feel homesick. That's what happened to me in Maine.

I asked the kids if it would be a good idea for us to move. I talked to my case worker at Catholic Charities, and she called the director of the Catholic Charities refugees office in Rochester. That woman told her that it would not do for me to move there because the community there was mostly single men. They had just come from Africa and they didn't have cars or anything. She thought that none of them would help a widow with children.

When my case worker came back and told me what she had heard from the woman in Rochester, I asked, "If we move there, are we still going to have what we have now—like medical assistance and food stamps?"

She said, "Yes, you can still have that, but you won't have transportation. No one can take you to the hospital or the grocery store as they do here."

I said, "I can walk. Let me just go there. If we still have medical assistance and food stamps, I need to go there."

She said it was my choice.

Rochester, Minnesota

—Mayor of Rochester Minnesota in 1996, during a special recognition.

—Barbara Bush during a visit to us at the Mayo Clinic when my sister was
admitted to the children's hospital.

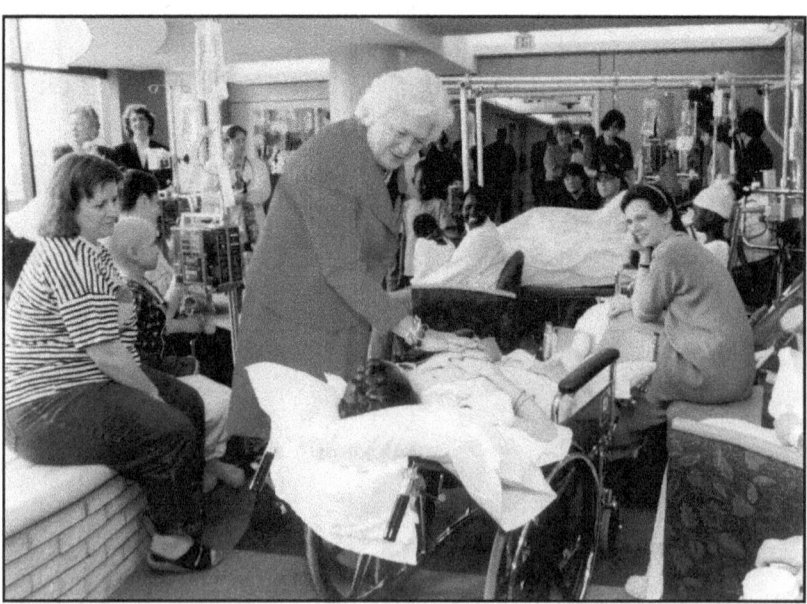

So we took the bus from Portland, Maine, to Minneapolis, Minnesota, in September 1994. Charlie March took us to the Portland station and sent a cooler with us full of drinks and snacks. I still remember him running beside the bus waving goodbye. Kut got lost at a bus station along the way, but a security officer helped me find him and we made it to Minneapolis. An American man named Jerry, who went to church with those Dinka guys, met us in Minneapolis and drove us to Rochester. The Dinkas had already found us an apartment.

Two days later, the director of the Catholic Charities refugee office, the woman who had refused to let me move there, called the Dinka men to her office. She wanted their help finding a Nuer speaker to help a Nuer woman and her paralyzed seven- or eight-year-old daughter, who were coming from Africa and spoke only Nuer. The men told her that the only Nuer speaker in their Rochester community was "the lady that you said couldn't come here—she came here two days ago."

The director came to me at my apartment, apologized, and explained that she hadn't wanted me to come because she thought I wouldn't get the help I needed there. Now that I was there, she accepted the situation. Then she asked me to translate for the Nuer woman. I said that of course I would, so we met the Nuer woman's flight. The man who was sponsoring her emigration was there with a large welcoming party of Lutherans from his church. They had met her flight with balloons and flowers, but none of them could speak her language. She was in tears at first, but as I spoke to her in Nuer she cheered up and smiled and was soon praying with her Lutheran hosts. Her sponsor, Mel Alms, later became my sponsor.

So everything was arranged by God. The Catholic Charities lady didn't want me to move from Maine, because no one would help me, but then when I arrive, she needed my help. I said, "Thank you, God. You are in everything before me." So I helped the Catholic Charities office with translation. I stayed in Rochester until Catholic Charities helped me. They helped me go to school to learn English. Mel Alms drove me to school and took me shopping.

I taught Mary, the Nuer woman, how to live in America. She needed even more help than I did—kitchen appliances, laundry appliances, bathroom appliances… We had to start from scratch. I taught her how to dial my seven-digit phone number, but I had a hard time doing it. One day she turned on the oven, thinking she was turning on a burner. When the water did not boil, she turned up the oven. Still the water didn't boil. She kept turning up the oven until her apartment was very hot inside. Then she ran to my place with her daughter, and told me her apartment was on fire. I sent Mareach to check on it. When we explained the problem to Mary, she said that she was through with the stove and from then on would eat at my place—whatever I cooked.

Mel drove Mary to her appointments and took her shopping, but they could not communicate, so I was always in the middle. He would call first thing in the morning to ask me to tell Mary that he would pick her up for an appointment. Sometimes Mary would not feel like going. I would argue with her over the phone. Sometimes Mel would have to come get me to argue with Mary in person. Back and forth he drove between his home, Mary's, and mine. Life with Mary was not easy for Mel and me. She needed more help than I was ever able to give.

One day Mel called to tell me that we needed to take Mary to the bank to open an account. We found Mary, explained what we were doing, and took her to the bank. She opened her account and deposited two hundred dollars. Then Mel dropped both of us at my apartment. After he left, Mary told me that she expected somebody to take her money from the bank. "How do you make sure nobody takes your money if it is not with you?" she reasoned. I explained what I could, but she was not convinced.

When my children started school, Human Services told me I had to get a job. Mary was so dependent on me that she was afraid to be alone while I was at work. That was when she produced the phone number of a cousin in Las Vegas. She had been carrying that number since before she left Africa. Mel helped her pack and move away to join her relatives. Before she left, we took her to withdraw her money from the bank. She had to admit I was right; it was still there.

Mary went to join a community of people who spoke her language and made her feel at home. That is how many of us are when we first move here. When you are not around any of your people, you do your best wherever you are, and then you move to be with people of your own tribe or ethnic group.

I stayed in Rochester because I had nowhere else to go. One day I told the director of the Catholic Charities refugees' office that I had left my siblings in a refugee camp, and nobody was with them. She helped me with the paperwork, and I sponsored them, and a year later, in 1995, my siblings arrived: Garang, Nyaluak, Bok, and Amor. That made nine people in my family. Amor was very sick in the refugee camp, so when she arrived in Rochester, we took her to the hospital. She had a seizure and was admitted to the Mayo Clinic with a brain tumor. She was there for three weeks. While we were there, Laura Bush, the president's wife, came to visit. I have a picture of her with Amor and me and some of the other sick children.

While I stayed with Amor in the Mayo Clinic, I wished I could get a job there because it was such a nice hospital. I prayed, and God heard my prayers, and I got a job there in the hospital as a dishwasher. My first day I was very, very happy to have a job. I could not speak very good English, but I spoke enough to have an interview and get the job. They showed me what to do, and I was a good worker. I did whatever needed to be done, and I worked really well. I had a good relationship with the supervisors and the case workers.

Most of my co-workers were young people. One day I noticed that they traded work times so they could have time off to do other things. I wanted Sunday off so I could go to church, so I took the necessary form to a young guy named Brian and asked if he could work for me on Sunday.

Brian said, "I don't give a shit."

I said, "Does that mean yes or no?"

He said, "I don't care." He filled out the paper for me, so I knew it meant yes, and I took the paper to the supervisor and had it approved. Brian and I traded hours regularly after that. Two weeks later, the supervisor asked me if I could work that weekend. I told her, "I don't give a shit." She was really confused and shocked. She called me to the office and asked me about it.

I said, "Oh, is it a bad word?"

She said, "Yes. Did you hear it in the dish room?"

"Yes."

"Who did you hear it from?"

I said, "I don't know," because I didn't want to get Brian in trouble. I apologized to the supervisor.

Back in the dish room, I told everybody what had happened, and they started laughing really hard. I didn't think it was funny, because I had said something bad to a supervisor. But the supervisor was a very nice woman, and she knew I didn't mean it. It was just a word I'd heard and thought it was a word that meant yes.

She became my best friend. One time I went to her house and cooked my Sudanese food for her and her children and we had a good evening there. I had a good, good time working at the Mayo Clinic. One year later I transferred to housekeeping because they had more hours, and then a few years later I transferred to linen and central service. I worked there as a tech and learned everything really fast, and I had a good time in the hospital. A few years later I was promoted to surgical services. I worked there as a surgical processing tech. I was doing a lot of sterilization and helping in the surgical area. I became a sterilization operator and did lots of things. I worked at the Mayo Clinic for almost ten years until things changed, and I decided to move to Lincoln, Nebraska.

In 1996 my two older brothers were stuck in Egypt. They had gone there to study and had finished their degree programs, and now they could not leave because of the war in Sudan. I found a phone number for Deng, the older of the two, and called him. We communicated back and forth for awhile. Then he wrote to Lutheran Social Services in Minneapolis, asking them to sponsor him. They replied that they could do so if he had a relative in the United States. Lutheran Social Services phoned me to ask whether I would fill out the necessary forms so they could sponsor him. I arranged for his case to be transferred from Lutheran Social Services to Catholic Social Services. After that, the paperwork went ahead pretty quickly for him and for my other brother, Jur, and Deng's wife, Monica. I had been separated from them for more than twenty years, so our reunion at the airport was a joyous occasion.

Now we had twelve people in the house. It was a wonderful house. Bringing all my family to the United States had been a very big project. I had no driver's license and had to walk a long way through the snow to sign papers. I felt like I had to do it because the war was still going on in my country, and my brothers needed my help. It was a big responsibility. Once we were in the same house together it was not easy. We had to take turns with the girls cooking. I was working at the hospital and was learning to drive because I had to take responsibility for my transportation and my children's. My brothers who came from Egypt helped with the children. When Amor got sick and went into the hospital to have a tumor removed, my older brothers helped a lot. They took turns with me giving her medicine in the middle of the night. I thanked God for their coming. Dinkas say that "the sister of brothers is better off."

We all had fun in the house. Jur loved to watch movies. We had no idea about movies, so he taught us to rent them. *Coming to America* was the first one we rented. All twelve of us gathered around the TV to watch it. Our second was *Lean on Me*. Jur was choosing our movies to teach us, and they helped us adjust to life in America.

My plan had been to bring over one sibling from each of my three stepmothers so that each branch of my father's family could be reunited. They had all been separated for years. Jur was able to bring his mother here. That stepmother came with two of my nieces, orphans, whom I had never met. (She calls me Saluk, because I came to America. It means something like *Deviant*. She means it affectionately.) Amor found her brother in South Sudan and sent money for his support. Garang found his mother, who had left him when he was four years old; he had remained with his father's family in accordance with our Dinka tradition when his parents divorced. Each of those restored relationships joined us to larger family networks. In that way, I helped bring the entire family back together. Even though some of the family remained in Sudan, we were reunited by phone and letters. I had prayed that my father's family would be reunited, so God heard my prayers.

By 2005, Atong had gone away to college at Winona State University in Winona, Minnesota. Deng had moved to Ames, Iowa, to continue his education at Iowa State University. Jur was married and busy with his family. Mareach had started college in Florida. Bok and Nyanluak were married, and Amor had moved to Minneapolis. I was left with the boys: Jok, Kut, and my youngest, Mathayo, who had been born in Rochester.

The boys had started hanging out on the street and flirting with trouble. I was tired from working at night and needed to slow down. In our Dinka culture, teenage boys need to be under the wing of their uncles on their father's side of the family. I had no one in Rochester to fill that role, but two of my husband's male relatives were living in Lincoln, Nebraska.

Lincoln, Nebraska

—Southeast Community College.

—Pastor Carl Godwin, good welcoming from
Calvary Community Church.

I moved to Lincoln and started to go to school. I did my nursing assistant
program here in Lincoln, and I had a very good teacher. I passed my test
and got my certificate. Now I am a certified nursing assistant. I found a
church, Calvary Community Church. People are really nice there to me.
Habitat for Humanity built me a beautiful house in Lincoln.

God cleared the way for me in his time. It was a time I was waiting
for, and God opened everything for me. Now I live here in Lincoln with
my children. My daughter Atong, in Minnesota, has just finished law
school and taken the bar exam. Jok and Kut have jobs in Lincoln. Life
is so good in America. God still has a destination for me, and it is still
ahead.

Conclusion

—Dinka men wrestling (If you look down, you will go down!)

My people say, "When you are walking, remember your back; think about the people behind you." I did that by writing this book. I feel like I'm planting a seed for my next generation. When they read this, they will know what we've gone through. I want them to know about our troubles with people in the northern part of Sudan, what they put us through. I'm happy that we have our independence, and I hope there will be no more war. Let there be no more dying children.

Lots of women went through what I went through, so let this book represent all of us, the South Sudanese women, widows and orphans.

Also, I wrote this book to honor my family, the Family of Tiir Angok, a branch of the Deng Kuol Family of Kuchdok; and all the Dinka Bor. Also, I wrote to honor the family of my husband, the Family of Kut Jok of Angakuie.

And finally, let this book be a memorial to all the people we lost along the way to independence. Not just my brother, my husband, and my daughter, but all the people we lost. This is a way to remember them.

Dr. John Garang De Mabior was a real hero to us, a Moses who led us out of the war. He died three weeks after the peace agreement, and his loss was devastating to us. We don't know if we will find someone like him again. He was from the Dinka Bor people, who lost as much as did South Sudan when he died. We all miss his leadership.

Conditions in South Sudan are uncertain. We are concerned with developing the country but must allow enough time for the situation there to stabilize. People there are enjoying being a free nation.

Many of the people of South Sudan were born into wartime. They grew up not knowing peace, not knowing love. Many lost parents and were raised by different families. Many make bad choices and cause problems for other people. For example, very young people ride motorcycles and cause traffic accidents. These conditions have implications for the future of the new nation. A populace that has no memory of peace will be hard put to recreate a peaceful environment.

Similar problems have come with us to the United States. Many of our South Sudanese children are dropping out of school without college degrees. They don't go back. Many parents must focus their energies on merely keeping their children alive instead of having the luxury of seeing to their educations and guiding them into careers, marriage, and family. Some parents are choosing to leave their adult children in the US and Canada and return to South Sudan. Many of those children who are left behind to wander by themselves do not do well.

My homeland is a Promised Land for me, and I keep thinking about going back. I keep going back and forth, visiting Bor Town and then returning to Lincoln. My heart is always in Bor.

I have bought some lots there and want to build a home. I applied for lots when they were dividing land in Bor Town, so I have five lots, one for me and one for each of my children. Last time I was there I built a small hut. I fenced my children's lots so people will know they belong to somebody. I was very lucky to get those lots in 2007. Now it is very difficult to get land, and people are fighting for lots. When I was there last September, I put gates on my children's lots, and my sister and I talked about them and agreed that we can rent out the lots to help me.

I want to keep my home here and my home there. My children live here. This is their home. So I am building a life here and a life there, while I am still a little bit young. So I will continue going back and forth.

In 2007 I was thinking of moving back to South Sudan, so I took my children there. The situation was still bad there, and people advised me to bring the children back to the United States. We came back and started life again. Now that we are here, I foresee having grandchildren and great-grandchildren here. It seems that I must give South Sudan some time before I consider moving back there.

-The time I visited with the former
Vice President of Sudan, Mr. Abel Alier.

This war of South Sudan left me with so many wounds. The loss of my brother was the first one, my husband was the second, and my daughter was the third. I wondered what I had done wrong. Was it a curse on me for failing to follow God's will? But I learned not to look at what had already happened, but to look at what was coming. Jesus was coming to forgive me of my sins. And Jesus came to me, and now I am a different person. Jesus healed my wounds. This is what I want to say about the situation now. One day I will meet them all again.

I keep thinking about and talking to people about how God helped me out of everything I went through. It was God, and no one else. He was sending me angels to help me with everything. We have an example. We wrestle a lot in Sudan. When you are fighting and you look down, you will go down. But if you just fight and don't look down, you won't go down. This is how it is when you are a widow. I didn't want to be a widow, especially in my 20's. You can be rejected by people. No one will like you anymore. You will struggle by yourself with your children. I didn't want to be a widow. But it happened. I was in God's hands. I put myself in his hands by my faith. Because of my faith, I didn't look down. I am fighting. I never looked down.

Thank you very much, and God bless you all. I hope my story will be a testimony that can help some other people to know that there is God ahead of us and everything will be just fine.

-The time I visited the children in South Sudan (orphans)

www.ingramcontent.com/pod-product-compliance
Lightning Source LLC
Chambersburg PA
CBHW070544290526
45790CB00002B/590